Casebook for
MANAGEMENT INFORMATION SYSTEMS

Solving Business Problems with PC Software

THIRD EDITION

David Kroenke

Sandra Dewitz

 Mitchell McGRAW-HILL

New York St. Louis San Francisco Auckland Bogotá Caracas
Lisbon London Madrid Mexico Milan Montreal New Delhi Paris
San Juan Singapore Sydney Tokyo Toronto Watsonville

Mitchell **McGRAW-HILL**
San Francisco, CA 94133

CASEBOOK FOR
MANAGEMENT INFORMATION SYSTEMS
Solving Business Problems with PC Software
THIRD EDITION

5 6 7 8 9 0   DOC/DOC   9 9 8 7 6

ISBN 0-07-035948-2

Sponsoring editor: Erika Berg
Editorial assistant: Jennifer Gilliland
Technical reviewer: Karen-Ann Kievit
Production supervisor: Leslie Austin
Project manager: Greg Hubit, Bookworks
Interior designer: Susan Benoit
Cover designer: John Edeen
Compositor: Susan Benoit
Printer and Binder: R. R. Donnelley & Sons

Library of Congress Card Catalog No. 93-79183

This book is printed on acid-free paper.

Contents

Preface to
the Instructor

The purpose of this collection of cases is to provide an opportunity for students to apply their knowledge of MIS and PC tools to solve realistic business problems. All of the cases involve computer-based projects (spreadsheet and/or database applications); each also addresses some of the broader issues concerning information systems and organizations. The emphasis in all the cases is business problem solving. Thus, although the casebook provides some keystroke instruction on using Lotus 1-2-3 or dBASE to implement case solutions, it is not intended to serve as a tutorial on using PC tools.

The MIS course is a difficult one to teach because it involves an awkward combination of topics. Information systems concepts are precise and concrete, while business and organizational concepts tend to be more vague and abstract. Blending these two into a coherent, well-organized course is tricky. The goal of these cases is to provide a framework for making that blend.

We have found that it is neither possible nor desirable to teach this course strictly using the lecture method. Some of the topics are not well covered by lecture. There are, for example, only so many ways that a teacher can say that information systems must reflect organizational objectives. At some point, the teacher needs to expose the students to a case situation (such as "Choosing the Right PC Tool for MHA") in which it becomes clear to the students, through the experience of analyzing the case, that, indeed, information systems must reflect organizational objectives. The students then understand that statement more fully than if they simply memorize it for the purpose of writing it on an exam.

Additionally, it is important to have a change of pace in the course. One lecture after another quickly becomes tedious and boring for both the students and the teacher. In this collection of cases, we have tried to develop computer-based assignments that provide interest and motivation for the student. By actively involving students in the analysis, design, and implementation of realistic—albeit small-scale—information systems, a teacher can give life to many of the concepts and issues in business applications of information technology. The *Instructor's Solutions Disk* suggests ways to use the questions and exercises at the end of each case, not only for individual and group projects but also as the basis for class and small-group discussion.

Origin and Nature of the Cases

All of these cases are based upon real businesses. The businesses have been disguised, however, so that both the positive and negative aspects of each story can be told without examining the real main characters under too glaring a spotlight. The cases show both competent and incompetent people; they show people with biases and axes to grind; they show confusion and distortion; they show effective and ineffective systems. Where possible, the issues of the cases are presented in the same order and manner as they were unveiled in practice. In some situations, this means the presentation of the issues is disorderly, but we believe that students will be well served in learning to disentangle the issues.

The cases cover a range of businesses and issues concerning a number of different industries: recreation, direct-mail sales, landscape design and production, and commodities trading. One of the cases concerns a nonprofit social services agency. The cases vary in level and sophistication. Some, such as "Evaluating Operational Policies at Jefferson Dance Club," are relatively simple and well-focused, and concrete and specific answers to the questions are possible. Others, such as "To Automate or Not to Automate: A Cost-Benefit Analysis for EPT," are more complicated and require more knowledge of business concepts and greater sophistication in the students' thinking.

MIS is a blend of information systems and business. Every information system is connected to one or more aspects of business activity. This means that there is always a need for knowledge about some aspect of business other than information systems technology. It would be a poor case that dealt only with information systems issues. Thus, we have developed the cases to address common business activities such as inventory management, financial analysis, cost control, marketing, and strategic planning. Terms specific to these activities appear in bold type; these terms are defined and discussed within the cases or exercises and are indexed in the Vocabulary Index at the end of the book.

Our Goals in Designing the Cases

The cases and accompanying discussion questions and application exercises were developed with three primary goals in mind:

1. to investigate a good blend of business and MIS issues,
2. to be flexible in supporting course objectives, and
3. to reinforce a structured approach to business problem solving.

We have sought to achieve the first objective by making the cases as rich as possible. These cases are snapshots of real businesses, and as such, they serve not only as cases for teaching students how to solve business problems with PC tools, but they also present many social and organizational issues, some of which are addressed as discussion questions in the case exercises. Most of the case assignments require students not only to use a PC tool to develop a small system but also to examine the human and organizational costs and benefits of such a system—for example, business effectiveness, efficiency, adaptability, innovation, and impact on quality of work.

To achieve the second goal, flexibility, we present a variety of cases and, wherever possible, structure the accompanying questions and application exercises so that you can "pick and choose" among them. For example, the case exercises for "An Inventory Management System for JKC" are structured so that you can focus on the database aspects of the business problems, or on the decision modeling aspects, or both; and you can choose to assign only a subset of the exercises, depending on how extensive you want to make the project. Or you can ignore the application development activities and use the case to discuss business process reengineering. Similarly, it is quite feasible to reduce the assignment requirements in a case such as "Evaluating Operational Policies at Jefferson Dance Club" by having your students construct only the baseline financial model. The *Instructor's Solutions Disk* suggests many ways in which you can tailor each case to your course objectives. A matrix of cases, key issues, and software assignments is provided in Table 1.

To achieve the third goal, reinforcing a structured approach to problem solving, we present the students with a four-step methodology (see "Guidelines for Solving the Cases") and have them apply this methodology as they develop case solutions. The case questions and exercises are structured to support the methodology by encouraging students to analyze multiple facets of the problem and to develop a good sense of what the requirements are and how they can best be satisfied before they boot the PC tools.

We want students to understand that the emphasis here is on solving business problems, not just on learning the right keystrokes or commands. Thus, a very important step in this methodology requires the students to evaluate the systems that they implement: Does the system satisfy user needs? Does it empower users to do their work more efficiently and more effectively? Does the system improve on old procedures or just "pave the cowpaths"?

■ Table 1	Case	Business Issues	Software Projects
Matrix of Cases, Business Issues, and Software Projects	Evaluating Operational Policies at Jefferson Dance Club	Effect of business policies on profits; financial modeling; employee relations	Construct a worksheet and perform What if...? analyses; create graphs.
	Choosing the Right PC Tool for MHA	Alignment of IT with business objectives; constraints in systems development	Construct a database; generate reports; compare SS to DB.
	In Search of ... Financial Planning at Starlight Expeditions	Operational and management control; strategic planning	Construct spreadsheets and perform What if...? analyses; create graphs.
	Improving Customer Service at WEB	Data as a resource for competitive advantage	Construct a database and generate reports.
	To Automate or Not to Automate— A Cost-Benefit Analysis for EPT	Business reengineering; resistance to change; cost-benefit analysis	Use a spreadsheet to do cost-benefit analysis of a telecommunications system; create a graph.
	An Inventory Management System for JKC —Parts A and B	Inventory management; business effectiveness and innovation	Construct a database; generate reports using view and report functions. Construct a spreadsheet decision model; perform What if...? analyses.

Using the Cases

As a general guideline for using the cases, we suggest that you assign the questions and exercises step by step and use a combination of in-class and small-group discussion activities and out-of-class activities for each case. For example, you can assign the Problem Analysis questions in one class period and discuss student answers to some of these questions in the next. Discussing these questions in class will emphasize the importance of the students' understanding a problem before they attempt to solve it.

Then you can assign the Design questions and have students meet in small groups during the next class period to compare their designs and work out some of the bugs. These small-group discussions are an excellent way for students to learn from each other even if they ultimately implement the solution individually. After the students have worked out-of-class, individually or in small groups, to complete the Implementation exercises, you can again discuss some of the Post-Implementation Review questions in class.

We believe that it is important to encourage students to work creatively and without detailed guidance from the professor. The students should assume that they are consultants who have been hired to answer the questions or develop the system for the businesses described. Clearly, in such a mode, telling the client that "I don't know what to do," or "I don't know what you want," or "I don't have enough data," or "This question requires marketing (or other discipline) knowledge that I don't have" is inappropriate. What would the students do if they were consultants? They would find out what to do, what the client wants, create a plan for obtaining the missing data, and find access to the required marketing knowledge. They might even guess or simply apply their own intuition, quite apart from anything they have learned in school.

Instructor's Solutions Disk

An *Instructor's Solutions Disk* is available for use with this casebook. It contains ideas for using the cases, background material on the business that was inappropriate to include in the case itself, and suggestions for answers to the cases. Additionally, there are several Lotus 1-2-3 spreadsheets and dBASE III+ data files and reports that provide sample solutions to the case problems. Contact the publisher to receive this disk.

Acknowledgments

Thanks very much to the professors who have used and commented upon *Management Information Systems* and the first two editions of the project casebook. We have received many valuable suggestions from these people. In particular, we would like to thank the following people for their ideas and suggestions:

Jerry Burstein, San Jose State University

Alan Heminger, Indiana University

Karen-Ann Kievit, Loyola Marymount University

Ranjan Kini, Indiana University

Tom Pollack, Duquesne University

Lazlo Pook, Metropolitan State College

Thomas Sandman, California State University, Sacramento

Tom Schriber, University of Michigan

Dennis Severance, University of Michigan

Glen Shepard, San Jose State University

Jill Smith, University of Denver

Anthony Verstraete, Pennsylvania State University

David Wellman, Wilson College

Carson Woo, University of British Columbia

Guidelines for Solving the Cases

The purpose of this casebook is to provide you with opportunities to apply the knowledge you have gained in your MIS course to realistic business situations. Each of the cases in this book is based on a real business. The names and details have been changed to provide anonymity to the businesses, but the problems, issues, environments, and constraints are all true to life. Many of the conversations recorded in this casebook occurred as written.

MIS is the awkward combination of technology and business. The combination is awkward because technology is precise, exact, specific, and concrete, while business is fuzzy, multifaceted, complicated, and difficult to assimilate. The development and use of effective information systems in business is an art. There is no algorithm or specific set of steps that will enable you to develop and use successful systems every time. Instead, systems are developed by applying intuition guided by experience and knowledge. The cases in this book are opportunities for you to develop your intuition and experience and to apply your knowledge.

Approaching the Cases

Approach these cases by first reading the case as you would read a newspaper article. Just read it for whatever interest it has for you. Then, read the questions and exercises at the end of the case. Read all of them even if your instructor assigns only a subset for you to answer. They will bring to light aspects of the case and perspectives on the events of the case that you might otherwise miss. Once you have read the case for interest and have read all of the questions, go back and read the case again for a deeper understanding of the facts, the problems, and the alternative solutions.

A common mistake in analyzing case situations is to jump to conclusions too fast, to look for a singular solution, and to oversimplify the situation in the process. In approaching these cases, strive to keep that impulse in check.

Instead, make every attempt to understand the business, its environment, the personalities of the people involved, the constraints, and other real-world factors before thinking about the problems and their solutions.

We encourage you to "Look before you leap" by structuring the case exercises and questions to follow a four-step problem-solving methodology:

■ **Step I: Problem Analysis**   In this step you examine some of the business and organizational issues raised in the case; you will also begin to describe the objectives and requirements of a solution. **Objectives** are the business goals the solution is designed to help the organization achieve. **Requirements** are the basic inputs, processing, outputs, and storage functions that the solution will need to perform to help the organization meet its objectives. The purpose of this step is to ensure that you understand the problem before beginning to design a solution.

■ **Step II: Solution Design**   In this step you specify the logical and physical design of a system to address the problem(s) identified in Step I. **Logical design** involves developing a conceptual model of the solution, independent of the information technology that will be used to implement the solution. For example, in a solution that requires a system to create, store, and access data from a database, the logical design specifies the kinds of data that will be stored. **Physical design** involves describing the solution in terms of the technology (e.g., the PC tool) that will be used to implement it. For example, here you would specify the **physical file structures** of your database. The physical file structure specifies the field names of each record, the type of data contained in each field (e.g., character, numeric, date), and the size or width of each field.

■ **Step III: Implementation**   In this step you use your design to develop a spreadsheet and/or database system to solve the problem(s) identified in Step I. Recognizing that you are not expert users of PC tools, we often provide pointers and hints to guide your implementation. In addition, the Appendix contains information about performing some of the more advanced implementation activities, for example, creating graphs from your worksheets and creating views and report formats for your database reports. The instructions provided are specific to Lotus 1-2-3 and dBASE, but, because the concepts are similar across products, you may find the appendices helpful even if you are using a different spreadsheet or DBMS.

■ **Step IV: Post-Implementation Review**   In this step you evaluate the system you implemented to solve the case problem(s). Does your solution solve the right problem? Does it meet the user's needs? Can the cost of developing this solution be justified by the benefits achieved? In hindsight, were mistakes made in analyzing the problem? Looking forward, what system enhancements or modifications do you recommend? No system is perfect; in fact, many fall far short, sometimes because of constraints imposed by the organization and sometimes because the wrong problems were addressed or only partially solved.

To facilitate your understanding of both business and MIS terms, we define a number of these terms. Defined terms appear in bold type and are indexed in the Vocabulary Index at the end of the book.

The remainder of this introduction provides additional suggestions on how you can approach these cases.

Consider Different Perspectives

A problem is a perceived difference between what is and what ought to be. Since problems are perceptions, they can, and usually do, vary among people. Further, people will have different objectives, both for themselves and for the organization. They will have different ideas about what should be. As you read these cases, remember that every person in the case has a different idea about what should be.

These different problem definitions pose dilemmas for systems development because an information system provides solutions in a structured, often rigid way. Information systems cannot (at least today) be as flexible and adaptable as social systems can. Therefore, when developing information systems, it is important to address the correct problems — ones that have the consensus of the group involved. To do this, the different problems must first be understood.

It may be easier to respond to a question or exercise if you take a single person's perspective. If you do, start your answer by defining that perspective and explaining why you chose to take it in answering the question.

Differentiate Symptoms from Problems

Oftentimes, the symptoms of a problem are more visible and obvious than the problem itself. It is therefore easy to mistake symptoms for problems. For example, the owner of a small business might define his or her problem as, "I'm not making enough profit." That fact is readily visible and obvious to the business owner. But is this actually the problem, or is it a symptom of another problem?

How might the business owner solve this problem? Profit equals revenue minus expenses. The business owner can decide to raise revenue, or reduce expenses, or both. This suggests a number of alternatives. Considering revenue, new marketing approaches can be taken, new channels of distribution can be opened, or new products can be developed. On the cost side, administrative costs can be reduced, the cost of producing the product can be cut, technology can be employed to increase worker productivity, and so forth.

By considering the statement, "I'm not making enough profit," as a problem, the business owner's thinking will be constrained. He or she might jump to the conclusion that employees are overpaid, for example. By considering it a symptom, the owner expands his or her thinking to the causes of the symptom and gains a much richer set of alternatives to consider.

Sometimes there is no cut-and-dried means to differentiate between problems and symptoms. Ultimately, the owner will rely on his or her intuition in deciding which factors are problems and which are symptoms. A concern for increased profit may lead to the need for new marketing approaches, which may lead to the need for new channels of distribution, which may lead to the need for a new product, which may lead to the need for different marketing personnel, and so on. Somewhere in this chain, the business manager will say, "Aha, that's it! That's the problem—that's the factor I want to change. If I change it, the others will fall into line."

The point of this discussion is to help you avoid leaping at the first factor that presents itself in the case. Instead, at each step along the way, ask yourself if you have identified the problem, or if there is not some underlying factor that contributes to the situation that is the true problem.

Be Guided by Your Intuition, Not by Available Data

In the questions, you will be asked to identify and suggest solutions to problems, to specify the nature of systems and their components, to relate systems to business goals and objectives, and so forth. Often you will be given data in the case description that is not relevant to the question posed. Do not make the mistake of attempting to use all of the case data. You often will not need it. On the other hand, sometimes you will be given insufficient information to form a well-grounded answer. In such cases, state the situation, make an assumption, or describe how you would go about obtaining the necessary data and what you would do with the data once you had it.

Assume you are a consultant who has been hired to answer these questions. The person who hired you may or may not know what data you need to answer the question. It's not that they're trying to trick you; they simply do not know or do not have the time to make a careful assessment of what you might need. They are relying on you to employ your knowledge and expertise and to ask for more data if necessary. In such a circumstance, it is not useful for you to say, "I can't determine the answer." Instead, your client will expect you to say, "I need the following data," or "I need to talk with the people in manufacturing," or whatever else you need.

In writing these cases, the goal was to describe businesses that actually exist, as they exist. There is no attempt to trick you or to manipulate you. Rather, the cases describe real-life situations as they appeared to the consultant who was involved. When confronting such a situation, you need to be guided by your own intuition and not by the data as it presents itself.

Answer with Appropriate Precision and Detail

MIS is a blend of technology and business. These cases and the questions that accompany them reflect this blend. In addressing these cases and in answering the questions, you will sometimes be asked to perform an activity that is very concrete and precise. In "Evaluating Operational Policies at Jefferson Dance Club," for example, you will be asked to create a spreadsheet to analyze the impact of alternative ways of compensating dance instructors.

On the other hand, you will also be asked to answer questions that are broad and imprecise. In the "To Automate or Not to Automate" case, for example, some questions ask you to determine a response for a business that has identified an information system that could potentially make the business obsolete. In that case, precise and concrete analysis is not appropriate. No matter how well designed, no spreadsheet can shed much light on such a situation.

Hence, when answering the questions, answer in a style that is appropriate to the question being asked. Do not attempt to answer broad questions with precise details, and do not attempt to make precise analyses with broad generalizations. Match the style of your response to the nature of the issue being addressed.

Use Your Creativity

Most of these cases or questions have more than one correct solution. Every one is different and is amenable to different solutions, even different types of solutions. The cases offer an opportunity for you to be flexible in your responses, in ways that go beyond traditional coursework.

Do not be restricted to the data and ideas in the case. Add from your own knowledge. Consider the remarks of the people in the cases; make judgments about their personalities and the credibility of what they say and do. Discuss these cases with relatives or friends who have business experience. Ask them what they think might happen.

Place yourself in the role of a consultant who has been hired to address the issues presented in the case. Assume that you have the authority to obtain other data, interview other people, and commission other studies. Where reasonable, make assumptions about data or facts that you do not have. Justify these assumptions. In short, be creative and have fun!

Case 1:

Evaluating Operational Policies at Jefferson Dance Club

Learning Objectives

The purpose of this case is to analyze the effects of various operational policies on profit and to learn how to use a spreadsheet to create models for financial analysis. Specifically, in this case you will:

1. Set up a worksheet as a financial model of a business operation.
2. Construct different models of the same business to test changes in an operational policy.
3. Graph the results.
4. Analyze and compare the results of the different models to make written recommendations concerning operational policies.

■ Spreadsheet Skills Required

Basic

1. Format a worksheet by entering headings and labels and specifying column width and cell type/format.
2. Write formulas to sum a range of cells.
3. Copy formulas using **absolute and relative cell references.**

Advanced

4. Replicate and modify your worksheet.
5. Create and print graphs.

We assume that students possess the basic skills listed above. Instructions on replicating your worksheet are provided in the exercises; creating and printing graphs is discussed in Appendix SS2.

Background

Edith, Rick, and Nancy are equal owners and partners of the Jefferson Dance Club. They were working as staff dance instructors for major studios when they joined together to form Jefferson. Their goal is to operate a dance studio that allows dance teachers to share in the revenue they generate. Thus, they offer each of their teachers thirty-five percent of the revenue they earn on private lessons and half of the revenue for group lessons. Additionally, Jefferson pays medical insurance for the instructors and provides quarterly staff training. During off hours, instructors can also use the studio to practice their own dancing, which is important, as many of them are professional competitors.

Dance Club Operations

Jefferson charges $45 per hour per student (or couple) for a private lesson and $6 per hour per student for a group lesson. As stated, instructors earn thirty-five percent of the private lesson fee and half of the group lesson fee.

For planning purposes, Jefferson divides the instructional day into two four-hour programs. The afternoon program runs from 2:00 p.m. to 6:00 p.m. On Mondays through Thursdays, the evening program runs from 6:00 p.m. to 10:00 p.m.; on Fridays, from 6:00 p.m. to 9:00 p.m.; and on Sundays, from 6:00 p.m. to 8:00 p.m. The Friday and Sunday evening programs are shortened because dances are held on these nights. No classes are taught on Saturday because the owner of the building uses it that day.

The number of private lessons given varies between the afternoon and evening programs and according to the day of the week. Figure J-1 shows the average number of private lessons given per hour for various days of the week and for both programs. Jefferson also operates up to three group lesson classes per evening. Figure J-2 shows typical attendance at each of these classes.

Jefferson has no in-house information systems. The company hires an outside firm to prepare advertising brochures and to maintain its mailing

■ **Figure J-1**	**Average Number of Lessons per Hour**					
	Mon	**Tue**	**Wed**	**Thr**	**Fri**	**Sun**
Private Lesson Demand per Hour Afternoon	3.0	2.5	2.5	3.0	3.5	3.0
Evening	5.5	4.5	5.0	4.5	5.0	4.0

Note: The evening program on Mondays–Thursdays runs from 6 p.m. to 10 p.m.; on Fridays, from 6 p.m. to 9 p.m.; and on Sundays, from 6 p.m. to 8 p.m.

■ Figure J-2

*Group Lesson Demand
per Class*

	Group Lesson Attendance					
	Mon	Tue	Wed	Thr	Fri	Sun
Class 1	10	20	15	10	10	10
Class 2	15	15	20	15	0	15
Class 3	0	5	0	10	0	0

Note: 0 indicates that the class is not offered that night..

list. Edith manually performs all bookkeeping, computes the payroll, and performs what little financial planning is done. The partners have talked about "computerizing" their business, but they know little about how to proceed, and they are not inclined to spend the money.

As this background indicates, Jefferson Dance Club is a fairly modest operation that earns an equally modest profit for the partners. However, the partnership is under a strain to generate more profit.

A Conversation Among the Partners

"The problem, Edith, is that we're not making any money in this business. We start with our revenue, subtract all the money we pay our instructors, then marketing costs, all our other expenses, then the studio lease payment, and we've got a small profit. But when we divide that small pot among us three partners, we have very little to show for all of our work!"

"OK, OK ... Look, Nancy, we've all been working really hard. We just finished the dance contest and show, and we're exhausted. Let's not get into this discussion now."

"No, don't put me off. I do want to get into this discussion now. In fact this is *exactly* the time to get into this issue. I'm making ten cents an hour at this job! We've got to find a way to make more money. I think the problem is that we pay our instructors a percentage of the take. When I think about it, we don't have three partners, we have a dozen! *Everybody* who teaches here is a partner."

"Rick, what do you think?"

"Well, Edith, I don't know. Nancy has a point. We do share revenue with the teachers. Would we be better off to hire instructors at a flat rate? We'd have to pay them less than they make now. But, at least they'd have a guaranteed salary. And, if we filled up their schedules, we'd make more profit. I don't know."

"I think we should focus on increasing our enrollments. If we change the way we pay our teachers ... Well, you know what will happen."

"Well, sure, Edith, we'd be more like the major studios and we'd lose some of our staff. But, would it be worth it in the long run? Maybe."

"Come on, you two. This is not the kind of business we agreed to start. We were all tired of working for a salary at the major dance studios and we said that we'd open a place and let everyone share in the revenue they earn. Give them an incentive. What happened to those ideals?"

"Edith, maybe the studios know something we don't. They have both fixed salaries *and* higher enrollments. I don't know about you and Rick, but I made more money as a studio staff instructor than I do now, and it was sure a lot easier."

■ QUESTIONS AND EXERCISES

Assume that you have been asked to help the Jefferson Dance Club partners analyze strategies for increasing profits. To do this, you will need to build a financial model of the various strategies. A **financial model** is a mathematical representation of a business's **gross revenues** (income from its products or services), **expenses** (the costs incurred to produce the products or services), and **net revenues** or **profit** (gross revenues minus expenses). After you have constructed a financial model of each strategy, you will write a memo, summarizing your analyses and recommending a strategy. Your final recommendation will need to consider not only "the bottom-line" but also the likely effects that each strategy will have on the Jefferson partners, their instructors, and their students.

■ **Step I: Problem Analysis**   We will begin by analyzing the Jefferson Dance Club's situation to make sure that you understand their problems and the factors in choosing a strategy to increase profits. Assume that you are to consider only the expenses related to instructor compensation and marketing to increase course enrollment; you can ignore expenses such as rent, utilities, and health insurance. The partners want you to analyze the effect on profits of the following scenarios:

1. maintaining current enrollments and
   a. paying instructors a percentage of the gross revenues
   b. paying instructors a fixed salary

2. increasing private lesson enrollment 50 percent and

a. paying instructors a percentage of the gross revenues

b. paying instructors a fixed salary

3. increasing group lesson enrollment fifty percent and

a. paying instructors a percentage of the gross revenues

b. paying instructors a fixed salary

4. increasing both private and group lesson enrollment fifty percent and

a. paying instructors a percentage of the gross revenues

b. paying instructors a fixed salary

For all scenarios involving increased enrollment, assume that ten percent of the *additional revenue* must be used to pay for marketing activities to create the increased demand. That is, you will need to add this marketing expense to your calculation of total expenses. You do not need to be concerned with any other expenses such as insurance or rent since they are not related to the teacher compensation plan.

Assume also that, for the scenarios that involve a fixed salary compensation plan, Jefferson will hire a sufficient number of salaried instructors to cover the maximum number of private lessons offered in the afternoon program. For the data in Figure J-1, this number is 4 (to cover the 3.5 lessons per hour on Friday afternoons). The salaried instructors will work both the afternoon and evening sessions and will be paid $500 per week.

Additionally, to cover evening private lessons, assume that Jefferson will hire part-time salaried instructors to augment the full-time staff. A sufficient number of part-time instructors will be hired to fulfill each evening's required number of lessons and will be paid $45 per evening. For the data in Figure J-1, for example, two part-time instructors would be hired for Monday nights (the four full-time and two part-time instructors will meet the need for six lessons per hour).

1. The partners have identified four strategies for increasing profits. What are the potential positive and negative effects of each strategy on each of the following stakeholders:

a. the partners

b. the dance instructors

    c. the dance students

2. What assumptions do you have to make in order to evaluate the feasibility and effectiveness of each strategy? Obviously, you must assume that Jefferson's current facility is adequate to accommodate increased enrollments. What other assumptions are necessary?

3. How can you verify your assumptions?

■ **Step II: Worksheet Design**   A spreadsheet is a good tool for analyzing multiple scenarios, i.e., for performing the kind of What if…? analyses required to investigate Jefferson's strategies. But, before you boot your spreadsheet program, you need to do some initial planning. The following questions will help you construct a plan of attack.

1. To begin, you need to create a picture of Jefferson's current financial situation. What data will you need to construct this picture? How will this data be manipulated (e.g., what calculations will you need to perform) to determine
    a. Jefferson's current weekly gross revenue for private lessons? for group lessons? overall?

    b. Jefferson's current weekly teacher labor expenses for private lessons? for group lessons? overall?

    c. Jefferson's current weekly net revenues or profit for private lessons? for group lessons? overall?

    d. Jefferson's current rate of return for private lessons? for group lessons? overall? **Rate of return (ROR)** is the ratio of net revenue or profit to gross revenue, i.e., profit divided by gross revenue.

2. Given the baseline model above, how will you manipulate the data and calculations to analyze each of the scenarios?
    a. maintaining current enrollments and
      i. paying instructors a fixed salary

    b. increasing private lesson enrollment fifty percent and
      i. paying instructors a percentage of the gross revenues
      ii. paying instructors a fixed salary

    c. increasing group lesson enrollment fifty percent and
      i. paying instructors a percentage of the gross revenues
      ii. paying instructors a fixed salary

    d. increasing both private and group lesson enrollment fifty percent and
      i. paying instructors a percentage of the gross revenues
      ii. paying instructors a fixed salary

3. Did you remember to include marketing expenses in scenarios 2b–2d? How will you calculate this expense?

4. The calculations to be performed in these analyses are fairly simple. But there is a lot of data to be displayed for each scenario. A greater challenge in this assignment is to determine an effective layout for the output of all the various scenarios. See Appendix SS1 for general tips on constructing your worksheet.

Assume that the Jefferson Dance Club partners want to see a breakdown of the number of private lessons, group lessons, and instructors for each scenario. This assumption means that you can't analyze the various enrollment scenarios by designing your worksheet to contain one financial model and then performing "What if…?" analysis simply by changing the value of an assumption input cell. Furthermore, as you'll see later, some of the exercises require you to generate graphs using data from the various scenarios. Thus, you need to have all the data for each scenario available in your worksheet at one time. What this means is that you will need to create a worksheet of the baseline enrollment scenario financial model and then replicate your baseline worksheet for each of the three enrollment increase scenarios, as illustrated below.

Baseline Scenario	50% Increase in Private Lessons	50% Increase in Group Lessons	50% Increase in All Lessons
• % of revenue • fixed salary	• % of revenue • fixed salary	• % of revenue • fixed salary	• % of revenue • fixed salary

a. Sketch the layout for your baseline financial model, including titles, labels and headings where appropriate. Plan to include both teacher compensation plans in this model. To facilitate replication of your financial model for the enrollment growth scenarios, include assumption input cells for the private lesson and group lesson enrollment growth factors.

b. What additional data or calculations will be required for the financial models in which you analyze the effects of increased enrollment? Again, to facilitate replication of your financial model for the enrollment growth scenarios, modify your baseline model layout to include these additions.

5. Now that you've planned the general layout of your financial model, you're ready to specify the physical design. Review your model layout to determine the column width, cell type, and cell format for each data element in your worksheet.

6. No matter how effectively you design your model, the partners will find it difficult to digest all the information and to compare the outcomes of the various scenarios. One way to increase understanding is to provide graphs that summarize information and make comparisons explicit.
   a. What information will the partners need to compare across the various scenarios?

b. Which type of graph would be most effective in representing each of these comparisons? Some common graph types and their uses are described in Appendix SS2.

■ **Step III: Worksheet Implementation** In the following exercises, hints are provided to help you construct your worksheet. Please note that some of these hints assume that you are using Lotus 1-2-3 to implement your worksheet. Also provided are some of the expected values—for example, gross revenues from evening private lessons—so that you can verify the correctness of your data and formulas.

Entering the Data and Formulas for the Baseline Financial Model

This portion of your worksheet implementation should be fairly straightforward, involving entry of constants for enrollment data and of formulas to calculate gross revenues, expenses, net revenues, and rate of return. You will need to use a combination of **absolute and relative cell references** in your formulas. For example, to calculate gross revenue for private lessons under the various enrollment growth scenarios, you will need to reference some constant data and some variable data in your formulas. Constant data, such as the $45 fee per student for private lessons and the number of hours per afternoon session, should be included in your formula as absolute cell references; variable data, such as the number of private lessons per hour, should be included in your formula as a relative cell reference.

1. After you have entered your labels/headings and enrollment data and have calculated gross revenue, verify the correctness of your data and formulas. The trickiest formula computes the gross revenue for evening private lessons, which should be $4545 if you performed this calculation correctly. If your answer is different, you may have misunderstood some of the underlying assumptions (e.g., about lessons per hour, hours in the afternoon and evening sessions); review your data and formulas to determine the error.

2. Now enter your expense data and formulas for each of the teacher compensation plans. Set marketing expense equal to zero in this no-growth scenario. Be sure to include appropriate labels and cells for entering the number of full-time and part-time teachers needed. A tricky formula here computes the expense of full-time and part-time teachers under the fixed salary compensation plan; this expense should be $2270 if you performed this calculation correctly.

3. Next, enter the headings and formulas to calculate the net revenue for each of the teacher compensation plans. If all of your data and formulas are correct, the computed value for net revenue under the fixed salary compensation plan should be $6445.

4. Finally, enter the headings and formulas to calculate the rate of return for each of the teacher compensation plans. If all of your data and formulas are correct, the computed value for rate of return under the percentage-of-gross-revenues compensation plan should be 63.24%.

Adjusting the Baseline Report to Analyze Enrollment Increases

Your next task is to repeat your baseline financial model analysis for the three enrollment growth scenarios.

5. Instead of reentering all your labels and formulas, simply copy your baseline model to a blank area of your worksheet.

6. Your next task is to modify your model title and the enrollment growth factor to reflect the scenario of this model. The following instructions assume that you are working on the scenario involving a 50% increase in private lesson enrollments.

   For this scenario, you will need to increase both afternoon and evening private lessons by a factor of 1.5. You could quite easily do this manually, but that would be cheating! Instead, locate your cursor in the cell for Monday afternoon private lessons, and enter a formula to calculate the increase. You'll want to reference the Monday afternoon private lessons figure in your baseline model and multiply it by the value in your enrollment growth assumption cell in this model. (Hint: Be sure to use your growth factors as absolute cell references in your formulas.) Now, perform your manual calculation of the increased enrollments to verify that the formula was copied correctly.

7. When you adjusted your enrollment figures, Lotus should have automatically adjusted your gross revenue figures. If everything so far has been performed correctly, the gross revenue for afternoon private lessons should be $4725; the enrollment and gross revenue values for group lessons should be the same as in your baseline report.

8. For the expenses section of your worksheet, you will need to enter the new numbers for full-time and part-time instructors. These numbers are used to calculate the teacher expenses for the fixed salary compensation plan. If your formulas copied correctly, your teacher expenses for the fixed salary compensation plan should be $3405. Also, you need to enter a formula to compute the marketing expenses incurred to increase enrollment, and then add this expense to teacher expense to calculate a total expense for each teacher compensation plan.

9. If your baseline model was copied correctly, Lotus should automatically calculate the net revenues and rate of return for the new scenario. To verify your copied model, check to see that the net revenue under the fixed salary compensation plan is $8772.75 and that the rate of return under the percentage-of-gross-revenues compensation plan is 60.72%.

10. Continue your adjustments, and repeat this process for the other two enrollment growth scenarios.

11. Print your completed worksheet. We recommend that you print it in four sections: the baseline enrollment analysis and each of the three enrollment growth scenarios. For information about printing worksheets, see Appendix SS1.

Generating Appropriate Graphs

Your final task is to generate appropriate graphs to illustrate the comparisons among the various scenarios.

12. Review your response to Exercise 6 in Step II; then create and print at least three graphs. Include a title, labels, and other identifying information for each graph. For information about how to create and print graphs in Lotus 1-2-3, see Appendix SS2.

■ Step IV: Post-Implementation Review

1. Does it appear worthwhile to increase private and/or group class enrollments? What recommendations do you have for the partners of the dance club regarding the enrollment growth profit-increasing strategy?

2. Comment on the results from your analyses of compensation plans. Is Nancy correct in her supposition that the Jefferson partners need to pay teachers a fixed salary in order to increase profit? What recommendations do you have for the partners regarding compensation plans? Discuss possible management and employee relations issues for the salaried alternative. Is the extra profit worth having to deal with these issues?

3. Which of the three strategies—fixed salaries, increased enrollments, or fixed salaries and increased enrollments—yields the greatest profit? the highest rate of return?

4. What other profit-increasing strategies might the Jefferson Dance Club partners have considered?

5. Prepare a written memorandum to summarize your findings. State the assumptions you made in performing your analyses. Comment on the results, referring to your graphs where appropriate.

Case 2:
Choosing the Right PC Tool for MHA

Learning Objectives

The purposes of this case are to illustrate the importance of aligning an organization's information technology with its business objectives, to examine the differences between database and spreadsheet applications, to learn the rudiments of database design, and to develop a small database and reports. Specifically, in this case you will:

1. Learn some of the important differences in the application of DBMS and spreadsheet products.

2. Examine three worksheets implemented to solve a tracking problem. Observe the **data duplication** problems of this approach.

3. Design a database that eliminates the data duplication problems.

4. Implement the database using a DBMS and create application reports.

■ Spreadsheet Skills Required

Basic

1. Create a file structure.
2. Enter records.
3. Write queries using single and **compound conditions.**

Advanced

4. Link two files to generate a report.

This case assumes that students possess the basic skills listed above. The advanced skill—**linking files** to generate a report—is described in Appendix DB2.

Background

The Metropolitan Housing Authority (MHA) is a nonprofit organization that advocates the development and improvement of low-income housing. MHA operates in a metropolitan area of approximately 2.2 million people in a midwestern city.

MHA serves as an information clearinghouse and provides three basic services. First, it works with politicians, lobbyists, and advocacy groups to foster the development of legislation that encourages the development of low-income housing through tax incentives, developmental zoning preferences, and other legislative inducements. To accomplish this, MHA provides information about low-income housing to state, county, and city governments. Second, MHA strives to raise community consciousness about the need for low-income housing through speeches, seminars, displays at conventions, and other public relations activities. Finally, MHA provides information about the availability of low-income housing to other agencies that work with the low-income and homeless populations.

Staff and Facilities

The agency employs a director on a half-time basis, a full-time secretary/administrative assistant, and a varying number of unpaid part-time volunteers. Both the director and the assistant are paid $20,000 per year. The agency is located in the basement of a building owned by a developer who supports the agency's work. Rent is minimal ($350 per month).

Finances

MHA's total budget is less than $100,000 per year. This includes salaries, rent, utilities, and operating expenses. The budget is supported by funds from several sources, including the state legislature, the city, a community services fund, and several businesses.

The director of the agency, Brenda Campbell, feels constant financial pressure. Each year she must reapply for funds from her sponsors. Considerable effort is required just to maintain the program. Further, she would like to expand MHA activities, but is unable to do so due to limited funds. Brenda estimates that at least one-third of her time is devoted to financial matters and fund-raising.

Brenda believes that a number of the businesses in the community might be willing to provide additional funds for her agency if she could demonstrate its effectiveness as an information resource. In addition to humanitarian concerns, she believes she can convince some of the community's businesses that helping her agency is a smart business investment. The logic in her argument is that, by helping MHA, they are taking a step in solving the problem of the homeless. Unfortunately, Brenda has been unable to find time to present these ideas to the businesses or even time to develop such a presentation.

Data

MHA maintains data about the location, availability, and condition of low-income housing in eleven census tracts in the metropolitan area. Within the boundaries of these tracts are approximately 250 buildings or other facilities that provide low-income housing. On average, each building contains twenty-five apartments.

MHA keeps data about each census tract, including geographical boundaries, median income, elected officials, principal businesses, principal investors involved in properties in that tract, and other demographic and economic data. It also maintains a limited amount of crime data. For each building, MHA stores the name, address, number of units, owner(s) name and address, ratings on several quality criteria (e.g., building maintenance, quality of service to tenants, heating/cooling system), and availability of facilities for handicapped people. In addition, MHA keeps a list of each of the units within each building. This list includes the apartment number, size of the unit, number of bedrooms, and monthly rent payment. MHA would like to maintain data about the average occupancy rates for each unit, but has been unable to collect or store such data to date. MHA does keep data about whether or not a given unit is occupied, however.

Information Systems

MHA uses an early COMPAQ 80286 system for word processing and spreadsheet applications. The system includes an older, but serviceable, dot-matrix printer. The word processing application is used not only for general business correspondence but also for the production of form letters using the mail merge facility of the word processing program.

The spreadsheet application serves two functions. The first is to maintain the MHA budget. Since MHA is a small organization with a modest budget, this spreadsheet is quite simple. The second function for the spreadsheet program is to maintain the apartment inventory data. As described below, MHA's experience with this application has been mixed, at best.

The Apartment Inventory Application

The Apartment Inventory Application is used to produce three reports about the nature and availability of low-income housing. Figure M-1 shows one of these, the Census Tract Report. As shown, this report lists census tracts, the buildings located in those tracts, and the apartments located in each building. The number of apartments and the average monthly rent payment are shown for each building, for each census tract, and for the entire region. (Figure M-1 shows only a sample of the MHA data.)

The second report is the Unit Type Report illustrated in Figure M-2. This report shows apartments listed by the number of bedrooms. (An efficiency apartment is shown as having zero bedrooms.) Within each category, the report lists buildings that contain apartments of that type as well as data about the individual apartment, including whether or not the apartment is occupied (A 1 signifies that the apartment is occupied). Summary data is included as shown for each building and category, and for the total.

The third major report, the Owner Report, is illustrated in Figure M-3. This report lists owners and shows the number of buildings and apartments that are provided by that owner. This report also shows the quality ratings for each building and a composite rating on each criterion for each owner.

This data is stored in a worksheet that was developed by one of the volunteers who works for MHA. The volunteer used a spreadsheet program because that was the only personal computer product she had experience with. She was unaware of the features and functions of database management systems.

MHA has experienced three major problems with this spreadsheet application. First, it is time consuming to prepare the reports shown in Figures M-1, M-2, and M-3. Second, these reports do not contain all of the data that MHA maintains and wishes to report. Data was omitted to reduce the complexity and time required to produce the reports. Finally, MHA personnel would like to be able to query their data on an ad hoc basis. This is impossible with the spreadsheet application.

■ **Figure M-1**

Census Tract Report
(1 of 2)

CENSUS TRACT REPORT

- -

| Census Tract Number | 10058 |
| Census Tract Median Income | $11,567.00 |

- -

Building Name   Elm St
Building Owner   D. Trump

Apt#	Bedrooms	Size	Rent
101	0	945	$175.00
102	1	1130	225.00
104	2	1311	425.00
206	1	998	220.00

| Total number of units | 4 |
| Average rent per unit | $261.25 |

- -

Building Name   Third Bldg
Building Owner   D. Trump

Apt#	Bedrooms	Size	Rent
202	1	1187	$188.00
200	1	998	176.00

| Total number of units | 2 |
| Average rent per unit | $182.00 |

- -

| Number of units for this census tract | 6 |
| Average rent for units in this area | $234.83 |

- -

■ **Figure M-1**

Census Tract Report
(2 of 2)

CENSUS TRACT REPORT

- -

Census Tract Number	10078
Census Tract Median Income	$9,879.00

- -

Building Name	14th Ave
Building Owner	P. Peacock

Apt#	Bedrooms	Size	Rent
30	0	1121	$271.00
20	0	887	105.00
10	0	667	158.00

Total number of units	3
Average rent per unit	$178.00

- -

Number of units for this census tract	3
Average rent for units in this area	$178.00

- -

Total number of units	9
Average rent per unit	$216.00

- -

■ **Figure M-2**

Unit Type Report
(1 of 3)

UNIT TYPE REPORT

- -

Number of bedrooms: 0

- -

Building Name	14th Ave	Building Owner	P. Peacock
Building Lender	Midwest Trust	Building Address	2700 14th Ave

Apt#	Size	Rent	Occupied Code
10	667	$158.00	1
20	887	105.00	1
30	1121	271.00	0

Total number of units of this type in this building   3
Total number of available units in this building   1
Average rent per unit of this type $178.00

- -

Building Name	Elm St	Building Owner	D. Trump
Building Lender	U.S. Bank	Building Address	123 Elm St.

Apt#	Size	Rent	Occupied Code
101	945	$175.00	1

Total number of units of this type in this building   1
Total number of available units in this building   0
Average rent per unit of this type $175.00

- -

Number of units with 0 bedrooms   4
Number of units available   1
Average rent for these units $177.25

- -

■ **Figure M-2**

Unit Type Report
(2 of 3)

Number of bedrooms: 1

- -

Building Name	Elm St.	Building Owner	D. Trump
Building Lender	U. S. Bank	Building Address	123 Elm St.

Apt#	Size	Rent	Occupied Code
206	998	$220.00	1
102	1130	225.00	1

Total number of units of this type in this building   2
Total number of available units in this building   0
Average rent per unit of this type $222.50

- -

Building Name	Third Bldg	Building Owner	D. Trump
Building Lender	U.S. Bank	Building Address	867 - 4th Ave

Apt#	Size	Rent	Occupied Code
202	1187	$188.00	1
200	998	176.00	1

Total number of units of this type in this building   2
Total number of available units in this building   0
Average rent per unit of this type $182.00

- -

Number of units with 1 bedrooms   4
Number of units available   0
Average rent for these units $202.50

- -

■ **Figure M-2**

Unit Type Report
(3 of 3)

Number of bedrooms: 2

- -

Building Name	Elm St.	Building Owner	D. Trump
Building Lender	U. S. Bank	Building Address	123 Elm St.

Apt#	Size	Rent	Occupied Code
104	1311	$425.00	0

Total number of units of this type in this building   1
Total number of available units in this building   1
Average rent per unit of this type $425.00

- -

Number of units with 2 bedrooms   1
Number of units available   1
Average rent for these units $425.00

- -

Total number of units   9
Total number of available units   2
Average rent per unit $216.00

- -

■ **Figure M-3**

Owner Report
(1 of 2)

OWNER REPORT

- -

Owner Name   P. Peacock
Owner Addr   13530 First Street, Suite 200
               New York, NY 10021

- -

Building Name   14th Ave

Apt#	Bedrooms	Size	Rent
10	0	667	$158.00
20	0	887	105.00
30	0	1121	271.00

Total number of units   3
Average rent per unit $178.00

Quality Ratings:
(Scale: 1-poor to 5-excellent)

Building upkeep	5.0
Tenant service	4.0
Heating/Cooling system	4.0
Pest control	5.0
Average rating:	4.5

Owner Summary

Total number of units   3
Average rent per unit $178.00
Composite rating   4.5

- -

Owner Name   D. Trump
Owner Addr   Trump Tower, Suite 2000
               New York, NY 10022

- -

Building Name   Elm Street

Apt#	Bedrooms	Size	Rent
101	0	945	$175.00
102	1	1130	225.00
104	2	1311	425.00
206	1	998	220.00

Total number of units   4
Average rent per unit $261.25

■ **Figure M-3**
_____

Owner Report
(2 of 2)

Quality Ratings:
(Scale: 1-poor to 5-excellent)

Building upkeep	4.0
Tenant service	4.0
Heating/Cooling system	4.0
Pest control	4.0
Average rating:	4.0

- -

Building Name   Third Building

Apt#	Bedrooms	Size	Rent
200	1	998	$176.00
202	1	1187	188.00

Total number of units   2
Average rent per unit $182.00

Quality Ratings:
(Scale: 1-poor to 5-excellent)

Building upkeep	5.0
Tenant service	4.0
Heating/Cooling system	4.0
Pest control	4.0
Average rating:	4.25

Owner Summary

Total number of units   6
Average rent $235.00
Composite rating   4.125

- -

Summary for All Owners

Total number of units   9
Average rent $216.00
Quality Ratings:
(Scale: 1-poor to 5-excellent)

Building upkeep	4.7
Tenant service	4.0
Heating/Cooling system	4.0
Pest control	4.3
Average rating:	4.25

■ QUESTIONS AND EXERCISES

■ **Step I: Problem Analysis** This case illustrates the importance of aligning an organization's information technology with its business **objectives.** Business objectives are the goals that an organization hopes to achieve; for example, one of MHA's objectives is to raise community consciousness about the plight of homeless people. This case also illustrates some of the constraints that can sometimes make this alignment infeasible. The Problem Analysis questions will focus your attention on both of these issues.

1. Review the reports in Figures M-1 through M-3. Discuss some of the inefficiencies in creating and storing these reports as worksheet files. For example, note the **data duplication;** if data need to be used in multiple reports, they must be entered and stored multiple times. What are some of the problems that may arise because of this data duplication (e.g., What updating is required if the rent for an apartment changes?)

2. As a nonprofit organization, MHA often has to "make do" with limited financial and personnel resources. Unfortunately, in this instance, having to "make do" greatly increases MHA's workload and reduces its reporting flexibility. Nonetheless, many individuals and organizations with far greater resources also sometimes choose the wrong technology for their purposes, perhaps because they don't understand how to align their information technology with their objectives.
    a. What are the strengths of a spreadsheet program? What kinds of applications is it best suited for?

    b. What are the strengths of a database management system (DBMS)? What kinds of applications is it best suited for?

   c. Many spreadsheet products support limited database functions. What are the differences between the database functions supported by a spreadsheet product and those supported by a relational DBMS product?

3. Review the case to identify the business **objectives** MHA wants to achieve through its Apartment Inventory System.

4. What input, processing, output, and storage functions must the Apartment Inventory System perform in order to help MHA achieve these objectives?

   a. Input:

   b. Processing:

   c. Output:

   d. Storage:

5. Why is a spreadsheet ill-suited to addressing MHA's objectives and functions? List the MHA requirements that are not met by a spreadsheet product but that can be satisfied by a relational DBMS. **User requirements** specify the functions a system must perform (e.g., input, processing, output, and storage) and the characteristics it must achieve (e.g., easy to learn and use) in order to help users do their jobs more efficiently and more effectively.

■ **Step II: Database Design**   Suppose that MHA is able to acquire a personal DBMS and a computer with a hard disk of sufficient capacity to store and process MHA's data. Further suppose MHA chooses a relational DBMS that allows data to be stored as tables. According to the principles of database design, each table in a database should contain data about only one entity or object. An **entity** is a person, place, thing, or event about which data is maintained. For example, in the MHA case, Building is an entity; each particular building, for example, the building named "14th Ave." is an **instance of an entity:** a real-world manifestation of the entity Building. (For a more complete discussion of these concepts, see Appendix DB1: Data Modeling.)

1. Consider the reports in Figures M-1 through M-3. List the entities represented by the data in these reports.

2. An **attribute** is a characteristic or property of an entity; for example, some of the attributes of the Building entity are its name, address, owner, and lender. A **key identifier** is an attribute that uniquely identifies each instance of an entity. The key identifier of the Building entity is its name. Thus, the Building entity as we've defined it so far can be modeled as

BUILDING

BldgName	BldgAddr	BldgOwner	BldgLender

Create a similar representation for each of the entities you identified in Exercise 1; list each entity's attributes, and underline the attribute that will serve as the entity's key identifier.

3. In a relational database, each entity is represented as a **table.** The columns of the table contain attributes of the entity; each row represents an instance of an entity, that is, all the data maintained about it. For example,

BUILDING

BldgName	**BldgAddr**	**BldgOwner**	**BldgLender**
Elm St.	123 Elm St.	D. Trump	U.S. Bank
Third Bldg	147 Third	D. Trump	U.S. Bank

Each cell (the intersection of a row and a column) in a table can contain *only one* data value. Thus, in the Building table, each row (building) can have only one value in the Owner column. If there are multiple owners, then the attribute "BldgOwner" must be removed from the Building table and a separate Owner table must be defined, as shown below.

OWNER

OwnerName	OwnerAddress	BldgName

The rows in the Owner table are associated with rows in the Building table by placing the key identifier for Building in the Owner table. Thus, for example, BldgName is added to the Owner table so that we can produce reports that include data from both tables.

Similarly, any time two entities are related to each other, the key identifier of one is placed in the table of the other. For example, the entities Building and Apartment are related in that a building can contain many apartments and each apartment is located in one building. Recall that each cell may contain only one value. Thus, we can't establish a relationship between the two tables by placing AptNumb in the Building table because each building will have many apartment numbers. Instead, we place the key identifier of Building in the Apartment table because each apartment belongs to *one and only one* building:

APARTMENT

AptNumb	AptRent	...	BldgName

Having established a link between the Building and Apartment tables, we will be able to produce reports that contain data from both tables.

Using these ideas, modify your tables as necessary.

4. Now that you have identified the data to be stored in the database, you need to describe the physical file structure for each table. The **physical file structure** specifies the field names of each record, the type of data contained in each field (e.g., character, numeric, date), and the size or width of each field. Your field names must comply with your DBMS's rules for naming fields. For example, in dBASE, a field name can be up to 10 characters long, must start with a letter, and can contain numbers and the underscore character (_) but no spaces or other special characters.

List the field names for each file, and then identify their field type and field width.

■ **Step III: Database Implementation**   You're now ready to begin implementing the MHA database. Use your chosen relational DBMS to perform the exercises listed below.

1. Following your physical design, create and save the file structure for each entity. Then enter and save at least 5 building and census tract records and at least 15 apartment records, using the data provided in Figures M-1 through M-3 as a starting point. You will need to make up some of this data because the figures show only excerpts from the three reports.

2. Sometimes a report requires that we access data from only one file. This is the case in each of the following reports. Query the appropriate file to print the following reports:
    a. The leader of a disabled rights group wants information about low-income housing for disabled people. Generate a report listing the building name, address, number of units, and owner of all buildings that provide facilities for handicapped people.

    b. The city welfare agency needs information about low-income rentals suitable for families. Generate a report listing the building name, apartment number, size, and rent payment of all unoccupied apartments with two or or more bedrooms.

        Note: This report requires you to write a query with **compound conditions,** that is, with two or more selection criteria. See Appendix DB4 for information about writing these queries in dBASE.

   c. A local politician has claimed that low-income landlords are not providing enough very low-rent apartments. Generate a report listing the building name, apartment number, number of bedrooms, and size of all apartments whose rent payment is less than $200.

3. Sometimes a report requires that we access data from more than one file. These times are when a relational DBMS really shines! As long as two files share a field (e.g., both Building and Apartment include the field BldgName), we can link them to produce reports that contain data from both files.

For example, assume we want a report that lists the building name, building address, apartment number, and rent payment for apartments with a rent less than $200. Note that this report is very similar to the one generated in Exercise 2c. The main difference is that it requires us to include data—building address—not included in the Apartment file. Thus, we have to link the Building and Apartment files to produce this report. For information about **linking files,** see Appendix DB2, or consult your user manual.

Link files as necessary to generate and print the following reports. *Note:* 3c may not require linking files if your database design includes owner name and quality ratings in the Building file.

   a. Brenda has received a request from the city welfare agency for information about small apartments renting for under $200 that would be suitable for one person. Generate a report listing the building name, building address, and apartment number of all efficiency and 1-bedroom apartments with rent less than $200.

b. A local politician has claimed that there are insufficient low-income buildings in the poorest census tracts. Generate a report listing the census tract number, median income, building name, and building address of all buildings located in census tracts with a median income less than $10,000.

c. A civil rights organization has charged that MHA is just a cover for "slum landlords" who charge high rents for poorly maintained facilities. To counter this claim, generate a report listing the building name, owner name, and quality ratings for each building.

■ **Step IV: Post-Implementation Review**   Now that you've created a small database for MHA, the advantages of a relational DBMS over a spreadsheet for this kind of application should be quite clear.

1. Summarize the advantages of a relational DBMS over a spreadsheet for MHA's Apartment Inventory System.

2. Are there any disadvantages in using a relational DBMS for these applications? For example, is a DBMS more difficult to use?

3. In what ways will your database system improve MHA's efficiency and effectiveness? **Efficiency** is a measure of how much an organization produces divided by how much it consumes; another term for efficiency is productivity. **Effectiveness** is a measure of how well an organization meets its objectives; effectiveness includes factors such as the quality of communication and decision-making processes. It has been said that efficiency is "doing things right" whereas effectiveness is "doing the right things."

4. Given that MHA is described as an "information clearinghouse," how will using a DBMS help MHA better meet its objectives?

5. Write a short memo (about 2 pages) in which you explain your database system to Brenda and try to persuade her to implement all MHA reporting applications using your system.

Case 3:

In Search of . . . Financial Planning at Starlight Expeditions

Learning Objectives

The purpose of this case is to examine how information systems can be used for operational control, management control, and strategic planning. Specifically, in this case you will:

1. Learn to extract relevant data about **overhead expenses, operating expenses,** and **revenues** from a case to set up a financial model of an operational business.
2. Modify the financial model to perform What if ...? analyses on course enrollments and food costs to explore the need for **operational control.**
3. Modify the financial model to provide **management control** (mid-season projections of profit and loss).

■ Spreadsheet Skills Required

Basic

1. Format a worksheet by entering headings and labels and specifying column width and cell type/format.
2. Write formulas to sum a range of cells.
3. Copy formulas using **absolute and relative cell references.**

Advanced

4. Create and print graphs.
5. Perform What if ... ? analyses by including an assumptions section in the worksheet.

We assume that students possess the basic skills listed above. Creating and printing graphs is discussed in Appendix SS2. The use of an assumptions section is discussed in the case and in Appendix SS1.

Background

Starlight Expeditions is a fifteen-year-old company that offers kayaking instruction and sponsors kayak and rafting trips down several major white-water rivers. Starlight is owned and managed by Robin Forsythe. Robin employs a secretary/office manager as well as a number of kayak instructors and raft guides. The instructors and guides are paid a per diem rate for the days they work. The raft guides direct white-water raft trips as well as operate support rafts that carry equipment and supplies down river. The base camp employs a cook and a cleaning/maintenance person. There are also a number of apprentice kayak instructors who are unpaid but who receive room and board when they are helping with a class.

Starlight's business is highly seasonal. The first courses and trips begin in mid-May, and the season is over by late August. During this period of time, Starlight conducts twelve introductory kayak courses, six intermediate kayak courses, and one advanced kayak expedition. Also, over the summer, eight rafting trips are operated.

Kayaking Courses

The introductory kayak course consists of five days of instruction followed by a four-day trip down the wilderness portion of the Smothers River. The students live and eat at the Starlight Lodge during the instructional phase. On the downstream portion of the course, students camp out along the river; food is provided and prepared by the Starlight staff.

Each introductory course is limited to twelve students. Except in unusual circumstances, such as periods of very cold weather, all the classes are at least 90 percent full. Food and supplies are carried down river on two support rafts. The raft guides help the instructors set up camp, and they also serve as camp cooks. The introductory courses are staffed by two paid instructors, one unpaid apprentice instructor, and the two raft guides. Food and lodging are provided to all instructors for both phases of the course. Raft guides receive meals for only the downstream portion of the course.

Intermediate kayak courses consist of five days of kayaking on a variety of sections of two rivers. Students in these courses live in a rustic resort lodge located near the rivers. All meals are provided by the lodge. Food and lodging are provided by the resort to Starlight on a fixed-price-per-person contract basis. Starlight includes the cost of food and lodging in the package price it offers its customers. Intermediate courses are limited to six students and are staffed by one paid instructor and one unpaid apprentice instructor. Again, both paid and unpaid instructors are provided with lodging and food during the course.

The advanced expedition consists of a group of eight to ten advanced/expert kayakers and two instructors. The duration and location of the expedition varies from year to year, but it generally involves a two- to three-week trip down a river on another continent. Participants meet in a departure city located in the United States and travel together to the put-in, or starting point, on the river. Food is provided for the planned number of days on the river. Hotels and transportation in the destination country are normally included in the course cost, although the specific policy depends on the country and varies from year to year. All travel, hotel, and food costs for the two instructors are paid by Starlight. Robin tries to plan these trips so that Starlight nets about $3,500 on the trip after all direct expenses (not including **overhead**).

Starlight provides all the necessary kayaking equipment for introductory students. An equipment list is shown in Figure S-1. Intermediate and advanced students are expected to provide their own equipment. Starlight will rent kayaks and paddles to intermediate and advanced students, if necessary. Students are required to provide all personal clothing and camping equipment, including sleeping bags, tents, mattresses, and so on.

Raft Trips

In addition to the kayaking courses and trips, Starlight operates eight 4-day raft trips down the Smothers River. Each trip consists of three rafts carrying six customers apiece plus a support raft that carries equipment and supplies. There are four paid raft guides.

Although the raft and kayaking trips are separately operated, they are scheduled to be on the river at the same time so that, in an emergency, the kayak and raft staff personnel can support one another. To facilitate cooperation between these trips, raft guides occasionally serve as apprentice kayak instructors and kayak instructors occasionally operate as raft guides.

Starlight provides all necessary rafting equipment for the customers. As with the kayak classes, personal camping equipment and clothing is provided

■ Figure S-1	Items
Introductory Kayaking Equipment List	Helmet
	Life vest
	Paddling jacket
	Paddling sweater
	Kayak skirt
	Kayak
	Paddle

■ **Figure S-2**

Schedule of Offerings

Introductory Kayak Classes		Intermediate Kayak Classes		Rafting Trips	
Class 1	5/12–5/20	Class M.1	5/12–5/16	Class R.1	6/14–6/17
Class 2	5/19–5/27	Class M.2	5/26–5/30	Class R.2	6/21–6/24
Class 3	5/26–6/3	Class M.3	6/2–6/6	Class R.3	6/28–7/1
Class 4	6/2–6/10	Class M.4	6/9–6/13	Class R.4	7/5–7/8
Class 5	6/9–6/17	Class M.5	6/16–6/20	Class R.5	7/12–7/15
Class 6	6/16–6/24	Class M.6	6/23–6/27	Class R.6	7/19–7/22
Class 7	6/23–7/1			Class R.7	7/26–7/29
Class 8	6/30–7/8			Class R.8	8/2–8/5
Class 9	7/7–7/15				
Class 10	7/14–7/22				
Class 11	7/21–7/29				
Class 12	7/28–8/5				

by customers. Figure S-2 shows the schedule of courses and kayaking and raft trips for a typical year.

Financial Management

Robin operates his business very informally. He has been in business for fifteen years, and he knows about what to spend for each course on equipment, supplies, food, and other expenses. He also has an intuitive sense for his personnel costs. At the end of the year, he totals his revenue, subtracts expenses, and determines what he has earned. He hopes to clear around $65,000 before taxes for the year. In the past five years, his actual profit has ranged from a low of $13,700 to a high of $87,500. Costs and prices for the current year are shown in Figures S-3 and S-4.

Every few years, when he makes more profit than he expects or when he feels he can otherwise afford it, he uses some of his profit to expand the facilities at the base camp. One year he added a new bunk house, the next year, new bath and shower facilities, and a third year, new vehicles for transporting kayakers and their boats. To set prices, he considers his profit from the prior year, assesses rates charged by his competition, and makes adjustments for inflation. Typically his prices increase from 5 to 10 percent per year.

Robin employs an outside accountant whose primary function is to ensure that Starlight pays its taxes correctly and on time. The accountant maintains a simple general ledger, but the ledger's sole purpose is to determine tax liability. No use of this accounting data is made for financial planning or for operational control. The secretary/office manager computes payroll and

■ **Figure S-3**

Cost Data

Labor Costs		
Raft Guides	$ 75	per day
Kayak Instructors	$125	per day
Cook, 6-month contract	$2000	per month
Maintenance person, 6-month contract	$1800	per month
Secretary/office manager, full time	$2000	per month

Other Costs		
Capital Equipment		
Lodge and attendant buildings	$275,000	value, assumed twenty-year life
Kayak equipment	$75,000	value, assumed four-year life
Rafting equipment	$125,000	value, assumed seven-year life
Vehicles	$37,000	value, assumed five-year life
Office equipment	$15,000	value, assumed five-year life
Maintenance and Supplies		
Lodge maintenance materials and other supplies	$5500	per year
Kayak maintenance supplies	$2240	per year
Vehicle gas and maintenance	$3750	per year
Telephone	$3500	per year
Office supplies	$2300	per year
Utilities	$3450	per year
Food Costs		
At lodge	$27.50	per person day
Down river	$33.50	per person day
Intermediate class food and lodging costs	$55.00	per person day

prepares accounts payable checks. Robin signs all checks himself. The secretary/office manager also receives incoming payments and records them on an income journal before depositing them in the bank.

Robin is not at all satisfied with this arrangement. He knows that his record-keeping is minimal and that he runs his business literally by the seat of his pants. He senses there are opportunities for increasing his profit margin, but he never has time to develop a system that would help him do this. By the

■ Figure S-4	**Prices**	
Course Prices	Introductory Kayak Class	$1250
	Intermediate Kayak Class	$ 995
	Advanced Kayak Class	varies from year to year
	Raft trips	$595

All prices include food and, where appropriate, lodging

end of the season, he is usually so exhausted that he takes six weeks off. Then he repairs Starlight facilities and begins his marketing promotion for the coming year. There never is time to improve his recordkeeping and financial management systems.

For example, for the basic course, instructors plan their own meals for the downriver portion of their classes. Over the years, different instructors have developed different methods and styles for preparing food. While the Starlight base camp cook has taken a role in ensuring that the meals will be complete and tasty, there is no real control over the cost of meals. Robin is certain that some instructors consistently use more expensive ingredients than is necessary. Additionally, some instructors are less careful about returning unused bulk food (large jars of pickles, for example) and thus cause unnecessary wastage. Robin manages this as best he can by checking the returned food, but often he has insufficient time to do this.

Most of the instructors are excellent camp cooks. Robin does not want to take away their opportunity to be creative in the planning of their meals. Instead, he would prefer to be able to provide each class with a budget for food and allow the instructors to plan meals within the constraints of the budget.

In addition to improved cost control, Robin would like to have a better sense of his financial position as the season progresses. One year he thought he was making a substantial profit, and so he planned that season's kayak expedition to operate at a loss. (The Starlight group was making the first run down a remote river in Peru, and he thought it would be good publicity.) He was chagrined to learn at the end of the season that he not only lost money on the expedition, but that his profit on other operations was at a ten-year low. He learned this in mid-September, a month after the season was over!

Another problem concerns the operation of marginally attended classes. Robin has a general sense that, for the introductory kayak class, it never makes sense to run the class with fewer than eight students. He has never really confirmed this suspicion with an analysis, however. And he has no sense for the break-even point for the intermediate class. Finally, Robin plans the expeditions individually, season by season, and so he does not see the need for a general financial model of those classes. He usually has a very good sense of his expense and revenue needs for these trips. His general goal is to make a few thousand dollars on the expedition, but if it nets good publicity, he's not too concerned. He does not want the expedition to operate at a loss, however.

Robin has also thought about offering bonuses to his more senior instructors at the end of the season. He does not know until September, however, how much of a bonus is appropriate. By then, the instructors have departed for other jobs, and he will not see them again until mid-April. In April, it seems ludicrous to offer a bonus for last season's work. He knows he needs to take some action here, however, because he has recently lost two very capable instructors to competing kayak schools in other states.

The Kayak Store

Starlight operates a small kayaking store in a shed adjacent to the lodge. It is a small-scale operation that grew out of the need to provide inexpensive but necessary items (suntan lotion, retainers for eyeglasses, baseball caps, etc.) to participants during the class. Invariably, someone would forget such an item, and one of the staff members would be asked to pick it up during a grocery shopping trip in town (27 miles away). Starlight began offering such items for sale as a way of dealing with this irritating, but real, need.

Several years ago, a salesperson for one of the suppliers of the kayaking equipment used in the introductory class introduced Robin to the idea that Starlight could begin to sell kayaks, paddles, paddling jackets and sweaters, helmets, and other paraphernalia to attendees. Starlight was buying such equipment at wholesale prices, anyway, and the supplier suggested that Starlight become a full-scale retail outlet.

Over the years, the operation has grown into a small sideline business. Robin sells equipment at an average of 25 percent markup. He estimates he sells about $35,000 (retail prices) worth of equipment on direct expenses of about $20,000. Often Starlight is not billed for the merchandise for a month to six weeks after it is received. In this time, Robin hopes to sell a substantial portion of it. He rolls inventory that is unsold by the season's end into the equipment inventory for next year's introductory classes.

Unfortunately, pilferage is a problem. He estimates that he loses 15 percent of his inventory to theft. One year he even lost two paddles and a kayak to theft! Overall, Robin thinks he nets about $15,000 on the store, not including overhead.

As with the rest of this business, recordkeeping is minimal. He verifies deliveries against order documents and checks invoices against deliveries. The office manager prepares checks to vendors. He keeps an informal inventory of items on hand and items sold.

Marketing

Starlight advertises in leading outdoor magazines. Robin also personally calls on popular kayak retail outlets in a six-state region that surrounds Starlight, and he explains the coming season's program. He follows up these calls by sending a schedule of classes. When a customer makes an inquiry, either in response to an ad or from another source, Starlight responds by sending a standard promotional packet. This packet includes a description of the courses, a schedule, copies of articles about the Starlight school that have appeared in outdoor magazines, a list of necessary equipment, and other related materials. The packet is enclosed in a glossy folder that shows beautiful color photos of classes on rivers. Informal feedback from customers is that the folder and packet are very effective.

Robin is satisfied with the effectiveness of marketing for the introductory kayak class and the raft trips. Each season he is able to fill almost all of the slots available, and he often has a waiting list. Starlight cannot expand the size or the number of classes and trips because they cannot obtain more permits from the Forest Service to take more people down the river.

Robin is not at all satisfied with the marketing for the intermediate and expedition courses, however. He believes that he has a marketing gold mine in the customers who have completed the basic course. When he has the time to call one of these customers, he is almost always able to sell them on the intermediate course. It's as if the customers are waiting to be called, to be reminded of the good experience they had, and to enroll in another class. In spite of this opportunity, Starlight does almost nothing with the list of prior students. In some years, Robin is able to send out a few Christmas cards, but this is done informally and without regard to any marketing strategy.

Business Opportunities

As stated, Starlight is unable to expand the number of introductory kayak courses and raft trips on the Smothers River. There are opportunities, however, to expand the number of intermediate trips and to offer more expeditions. In fact, Starlight could double or triple the number of intermediate courses.

Considering the expeditions, the high level of skill required of participants limits the size of the market. It would be possible, however, for Starlight to offer international trips on rivers that involve easier kayaking. In fact, Robin has been approached on several occasions by kayaking schools in other countries to offer classes on a joint basis. In this regard, Starlight would use its customer base to generate demand for trips that are operated by other companies in other countries. Such an arrangement would allow Starlight to take advantage of its extensive customer list and would provide the other companies with a stream of qualified kayakers.

Other opportunities involve opening new schools on other rivers. On occasion, Robin has discussed this possibility with some of his senior instructors. In fact, one of his instructors, Rose Darlia, has proposed opening a school on a partnership basis with Starlight. According to her proposal, Starlight would provide advice, assistance, and $50,000, and it would co-sign on a line of credit to start the new business. Further, Starlight and the new school would share marketing activities and expenses. Also, the two schools could refer customers to one another when classes become full.

Finally, Robin knows that about 40 percent of the graduates of the introductory class continue kayaking. As such, his customer base reflects a target market for direct mail sales of kayaking equipment and supplies. In fact, on an informal basis, he occasionally sells kayaks and other large-dollar items to prior students when they approach him. He has thought about expanding this into a full-scale direct mail company. He knows that he has the confidence of his course graduates.

If Starlight were to endorse one or two products as being well suited for particular tasks, and if they were to provide an attractive price, he believes they would be able to generate substantial sales. Doing so would enable him to provide year-round work for some of the kayaking personnel.

Robin would like to consider all of these proposals further, but he has not been able to find the time to do so.

■ QUESTIONS AND EXERCISES

What a mess! Robin seems to have lots of good ideas and plans, but too little time to follow through on any of them. He has hired you as a business consultant; your job is to (1) analyze his current financial situation, (2) project the impact of varying food costs and demand levels on profitability, (3) suggest ways to use information technology to improve his operational and management control, and (4) evaluate the feasibility of some of his strategic opportunities.

To perform these exercises, you need a basic familiarity with three primary processes that organizations perform: operational control, management control, and strategic planning. **Operational control** is the process of controlling the day-to-day activities of an organization; it includes activities such as sales order processing and inventory control. **Management control** is the process of ensuring that the organization's resources are obtained and used efficiently and effectively; management control activities include procurement and personnel management. **Strategic planning** is the process of defining the organization's goals and ensuring its survival and growth; strategic planning activities include deciding to open branch offices or to build a new manufacturing plant or to develop a new product.

■ Step I: Problem Analysis

1. Review the case to identify areas in which Robin has failed to manage his business effectively, for example, areas in which he has ignored basic **operational and management control** needs and has not performed adequate **strategic planning.** How might Robin's mismanagement endanger his business survival?

2. Robin is paying to have a business consultant analyze his business. This act suggests that he wants to improve the way his business operates. What business **objectives** does Robin hope to achieve as a result of your analysis? Objectives are the goals that a business sets for itself. For example, in the Starlight case, it's fairly obvious that one business objective is to *improve*—or at least ensure—*the profitability of Starlight Expeditions.* What are Robin's other business objectives?

3. Robin has mentioned several ideas and plans for improving the way that Starlight Expeditions is managed and for taking advantage of expansion opportunities. Review the case, making a list of these ideas. Then classify them as operational control issues, management control issues, or strategic planning issues; some of Robin's ideas may address multiple issues.

4. What information do you as a consultant need to analyze Starlight's current financial position? Is all this information provided in the case? If not, what additional information is needed, and how can you obtain it?

5. Consider the financial model that you will build to perform your analysis. A **financial model** is a mathematical representation of a business's gross revenues, expenses, and net revenue or profit. **Gross revenue,** or simply revenue, is the money generated from an activity. **Expenses** are the costs of performing a business activity. Expenses are generally one of two types. **Operating expenses** are expenses directly related to a particular business activity. For example, the payroll, food, and lodging costs for the raft guides and kayak instructors are operating expenses directly related to providing the kayak courses and raft trips. **Overhead expenses** are the general expenses of running a business that cannot be directly attributed to a particular business activity. For example, the costs associated with Starlight's lodge cannot be directly assigned to a particular course; these are expenses related to many of the services Starlight provides. **Net revenue** or **profit** is gross revenue minus expenses.

What data must be input into the Starlight financial model? What kinds of processing must the model perform? What outputs must it generate?

■ **Step II: Worksheet Design** Assume that Robin wants you to answer the following questions about Starlight's operations:

- Given the current operating expense, overhead, and revenue data, if all classes are full, what is Starlight's projected net revenue (profit)?

- How sensitive is Starlight's profit to changes in class size? Assume that classes are 70, 80, 90, and 100 percent full.

- How sensitive is Starlight's profit to changes in food costs for the introductory course and raft trips? Assume that these costs are 80, 100, 120, and 140 percent of the costs shown in Figure S-3.

- Assuming that all courses and trips are fully enrolled, what percentage of gross revenue does each activity contribute to Starlight's total gross revenue?

- How should overhead expenses be allocated to each revenue-generating activity?

Answering these questions will require you to build a financial model of Starlight Expeditions. In this section, we focus on designing the financial model for the baseline scenario, assuming 100 percent enrollment and 100 percent food costs.

A spreadsheet is a good tool for building a financial model and for analyzing multiple scenarios. But, before you boot your spreadsheet program, you need to do some initial planning. The questions here will help you devise a plan. The calculations to be performed in these analyses are fairly simple. A greater challenge is determining an effective layout for your financial model, given the number of inputs, calculations, and outputs that must be included.

There are a number of ways that you could design a worksheet to analyze

Starlight's finances. Although there is no single correct design for your worksheet, some designs are better than others. Here, we encourage you to organize your worksheet into major sections for gross revenue, expenses, and net revenue, each containing subsections for Starlight's various revenue-generating activities. We assume that the calculation of overhead expenses and the calculation of the portion of total overhead expense to allocate to each activity are presented in a separate section of your worksheet. Appendix SS1 provides information on how to design a worksheet.

1. To begin, you need to identify all of Starlight's sources of revenue, assuming that all courses and raft trips are fully enrolled. What data will you need and how will you manipulate this data to determine Starlight's current **gross revenue** for introductory kayak courses? For intermediate kayak courses? For raft trips? For the store? Overall?

2. Review Figure S-3 and the case to classify Starlight's expenses as (a) operating expenses or (b) overhead expenses. We will deal with overhead expenses later. What data will you need and how will this data be manipulated to determine Starlight's current **operating expenses** for introductory kayak courses? For intermediate kayak courses? For raft trips? For the store? Overall?

3. How will you calculate Starlight's current **net revenue/profit** (before overhead expenses have been subtracted) for introductory kayak courses? For intermediate kayak courses? For the expedition? For raft trips? For the store? Overall?

4. How will you incorporate **overhead expenses?** As a separate worksheet? As a section of your financial model? Keep in mind that, after you have calculated gross revenue, operating expenses, and net revenue, you will need to allocate overhead expenses to each activity; thus, it may be best to include overhead expenses as a section of your financial model.

Recall that overhead expenses are not directly attributable to a particular business activity. One formula you can use to allocate a portion of total overhead expense to each activity is

$$Activity\ Overhead = (Activity\ Revenue/Total\ Revenue) \times Total\ Overhead$$

5. Now that you've planned the general layout of your financial model, you're ready to specify the physical design. Review your layout to determine the column width, cell type (e.g., character, numeric, formula), and cell format (e.g., left-justified, currency, percentage) for each data element in your worksheet.

■ **Step III: Implementation**   In the following exercises, hints are provided to help you write some of the more complex formulas. Please note that these hints assume that you are using Lotus 1-2-3 to implement your worksheet. If you are using another product, please consult that product's user manual. Because many spreadsheet products employ similar functions and features, the Lotus hints should help you even if you are using a different product (e.g., Microsoft Excel). But, just to be safe, *consult your user manual!*

A. *Implementing the Baseline Financial Model*

Gross Revenues

1. Review your worksheet layout design for gross revenue. Enter your labels and column headings, and format your worksheet with the column widths, cell types, and cell formats specified in your worksheet layout design.

2. Enter the revenue data, assuming that all courses and trips are fully enrolled. In the appropriate cells, write formulas to calculate the gross revenue from each activity and the total gross revenue. Verify your data and formulas by checking to see that total gross revenue from all sources (not including the expedition and assuming 100% enrollment) is $336,500.

Operating Expenses

3. Review your worksheet layout design for operating expenses. Enter your labels and column headings, and format your worksheet with the column widths, cell types, and cell formats specified in your worksheet layout design.

4. Enter the operating expense data, assuming the payroll, lodging, and food costs shown in Figure S-3. In the appropriate cells, write formulas to calculate the operating expenses for each activity and the total operating expenses, assuming that all classes are full. Verify your data and formulas by checking to see that total operating expense is $156,420.

Annual Overhead Expense

5. Review your worksheet layout design for annual overhead expenses. Enter your labels and column headings, and format your worksheet with the column widths, cell types, and cell formats specified in your worksheet layout design.

6. Enter the overhead expense data. In the appropriate cells, write formulas to calculate the annual cost of each overhead item and Starlight's total annual overhead expense. Verify your data and formulas by checking to see that total annual overhead expense is $128,297.

Allocation of Overhead Expense

7. Review your worksheet layout design for allocation of overhead expense. Using the 100 percent enrollment gross revenue data, determine the allocation of overhead expense to each of Starlight's revenue-generating activities. Recall that the overhead allocated to each activity is determined using the following formula:

   (Activity Gross Revenue/ Total Gross Revenue) × Total Overhead Expense

8. Assuming that you performed the overhead allocation calculations in another section of your worksheet, transfer the overhead expense for each activity to the expenses section of your worksheet. Sum the operating and overhead expenses for each activity to show Starlight's total expenses.

Net Revenue

9. Review your worksheet layout design for net revenues. Enter your labels and column headings, and format your worksheet with the column widths, cell types, and cell formats specified in your worksheet layout design.

10. In the appropriate cells, write formulas to calculate the net revenue after overhead has been subtracted for each activity and the total net revenue. Verify your data and formulas by checking to see that total net revenue from all income-generating activities is $55,283, assuming 100 percent food costs and 100 percent enrollment.   *OK*

B.   Modifying Your Worksheet for the Various Scenarios

One of your tasks is to analyze the sensitivity of Starlight's profits to the demand for courses and trips and to the cost of food. To perform this analysis, you will need to modify your baseline financial model to include columns for the 70, 80, and 90 percent enrollment assumptions in the gross revenues section and for the 80, 120, and 140 percent food costs in your expenses section. To analyze Starlight's gross revenue, expenses, and net revenue under various scenarios, you will need to include assumption data in each section. Appendix SS1 provides information on how to design a worksheet.

You will need to use a combination of **absolute and relative cell references** in your formulas. For example, to calculate gross revenue for raft trips under the various enrollment percentages, you will need to reference some constant data and some variable data in your formulas. Constant data, such as the $595 fee per student for raft trips and the number of trips per year, should be included in your formula as absolute cell references; variable data, such as the number of customers on each raft trip, should be included in your formula as a relative cell reference.

11. Modify your gross revenues section to include columns to determine gross revenues assuming that introductory and intermediate classes and raft trips are 70, 80, and 90 percent full. In the appropriate cells, write formulas to calculate the gross revenue from each activity under each enrollment scenario and the total gross revenue.

12. Modify your expenses section to include columns to determine operating expenses, assuming that food costs for raft trips and introductory courses are 80, 120, and 140 percent of the costs shown in Figure S-3.

13. Modify your net revenues section to display the net revenues under the various scenarios. In the appropriate cells, write formulas to calculate the net revenue for each activity and the total net revenue under the following conditions:
    a. assuming that food costs are 100 percent and that classes and trips are 70, 80, and 90 percent full.

    b. assuming that all classes and trips are 100 percent full and that food costs are 80, 100, 120, and 140 percent of the food costs given in Figure S-3.

C.   *Creating Graphs to Illustrate Your Analysis*

See Appendix SS2 for information about creating and printing graphs.

14.   Using the model developed in the exercises for Part A, graph total gross revenue to show the percentage contributed by each income-generating activity, assuming that all classes and trips are full and that food costs are 100 percent.   *pie chart*

15.   Create a graph to compare profitability across the enrollment scenarios, assuming food costs are 100 percent.

16.   Create a graph to compare profitability across the food cost scenarios, assuming enrollment is 100 percent.

D.   *Modifying the Model to Provide Management Control*

17.   Extend the model you developed in the exercises for Part A to allow Robin or his assistant to enter actual enrollments and operating expenses as they occur. Design your worksheet to show the differences between actual and budgeted amounts for each operating expense for each course and the amount remaining of each budgeted expense's annual budget.

■ Step IV: Post-Implementation Review

1. Reflect on the results of your financial analysis. What implications do these results have for the management of Starlight? How sensitive is Starlight's profit to demand for classes? To food costs? **Sensitivity** here refers to how dependent Starlight's profit is on course enrollment and food costs; for example, if a small reduction in enrollment or a small increase in food costs has a significant impact on Starlight's profitability, then Starlight's profit is very sensitive to these factors.

2. Prepare a short memo (about 2 pages) to Robin summarizing the results of your analyses and their implications. Refer to your graphs as appropriate.

3. Figure S-5 shows three ways in which information systems can add value to an organization. Using this figure as a guide, assess the potential role of information systems at Starlight. Describe business functions that could be facilitated by information systems. Briefly describe the features and functions that the systems would provide.

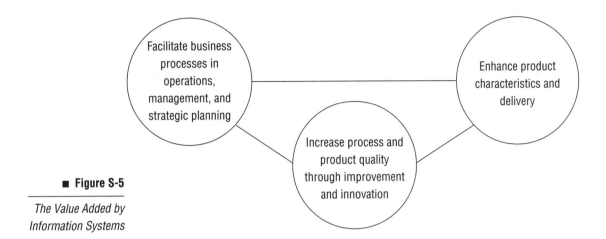

■ **Figure S-5**

The Value Added by Information Systems

4. How might an information system help Robin allocate staff bonuses? Consider ways that information systems could be used to assess the contributions of each instructor to the success of Starlight. How should the bonus program be related to Starlight's overall profitability?

5. Considering what you know about Robin, what is the likelihood that he will implement any of your recommendations?

Case 4:
Improving Customer Service at WEB

Learning Objectives

The purpose of this case is to illustrate how information technology can be used to improve customer service by helping an organization maintain data and tailor its marketing to serve customer needs more effectively. Specifically, in this case you will:

1. Understand how data can be used as a resource to give a firm a **competitive advantage.**
2. Analyze the customer data needs of a firm.
3. Use a DBMS to construct a database and generate reports.
4. Use a DBMS to create a **report format file** for frequently generated reports.

■ Database Skills Required

Basic

1. Create a file structure.
2. Enter records for each file.
3. Write queries using single and **compound conditions.**
4. **Sort** a file on a sort key.
5. **Link files** and create **views** to generate a report.

Advanced

6. Create and use a **report format** to generate a report.
7. Create and use a **label format file** to generate mailing labels.

We assume that students already possess all the basic database skills listed above. Linking files and creating report formats are discussed in Appendices DB2 and DB3, respectively. Creating a labels file is discussed in Appendix DB4.

Background

William Ellison sells rare books, manuscripts, and first editions. Although he works for a large bookseller in the United States, he is known throughout the world for his ability to locate and sell rare manuscripts. William is successful, in large measure, because he has a prodigious memory, speaks seven languages, and maintains relationships with numerous serious book dealers and customers on all continents. In fact, his knowledge is so vast that the world's museums and libraries consult him regarding the location or possible location of rare items. William constantly culls his sources to learn of the existence and location of rare works. Once a month, he publishes the results of his work in a newsletter that describes materials that he has purchased or can obtain. In the latter case, he charges a commission for serving as a broker between the buyer and seller.

Customer Tracking

The primary key to William's success is his extensive client base. Whenever he receives an order or inquiry from a new client, William records the client's name, address, phone number, and interest on a sheet of paper and adds a folder marked with the customer's name to his customer file. (See Figure E-1 for sample customer data.) Currently, William's customer file includes almost 2500 customers. William notes all customer purchases and inquiries in the customer folder; he also keeps track of any other contacts with each customer, such as telephone conversations conducted and letters sent. William would like to be able to process his customer file to identify who his best buyers are, but reviewing all the customer folders, which fill two four-drawer file cabinets, has become an impossible task.

Instead, each quarter, William reviews his orders file to identify customers who have made a purchase, and then he sends customized letters to these customers. Typically, he writes three or four different types of letter and sends one or another of them to a customer, depending on the purchases that a customer has made. When he can, he refers, by name, to a recent purchase. For example, he might start a letter with a sentence like "I hope you're enjoying the *Huckleberry Finn* First Edition," and then continue to mention a related product. William feels that this is a successful marketing tactic, but has been unable to verify this belief because of the extensive labor that would be involved in reviewing all of his customer records to relate marketing letters sent to purchases made. In addition, William is concerned that, because he sends letters only to customers who have recently made a purchase, he may be ignoring a potential gold mine—the hundreds of customers who did not make a purchase during that quarter.

ID	Name	Address	Phone	Interest
B114	Marilyn Baker	31 James Woods Ct, Manchester, England	011-0522-75 88 99	Child Lit
C067	Frank Charles	31762 N. Sunset, Los Angeles, CA 96666	(213) 757-8800	SciFi
D322	William Doyle	2943 Cordell Ave, Cleveland, OH 44113	(216) 779-5050	19th Cent Am.
K142	Kenneth King	485 High St, Victoria 3181 Australia	061-0347-88 42 17	20th Cent Am.
L261	Steve Lawrence	Castle St, Salisbury, Wiltshire, England	011-7033-90 75 22	Child Lit
P116	Stone Phillips	65 George St, Edinburgh EH2 2JL UK	044-0311-87 09 66	Modern
S264	James Stargardt	Rade-Strasse 10, Hamburg, Germany	049-4033-69 90 22	19th Cent Am.
T183	Jean Toulouse	Place du Casino, Monaco 98001	033-9901-76 89 71	20th Cent Am.

■ **Figure E-1**

Sample Customers

To maintain at least some degree of contact with all his customers, William mails newsletters to every customer each month. For years, William kept his mailing list in a file of 3-by-5 cards. A number of years ago, when the expense of addressing over 2000 newsletters had become excessive, he hired a service bureau (an independent company that provides computer processing services) to process the mailing list. They made several mistakes, however, and William received many of his newsletters back as undeliverable. This he found inexcusable. Just recently he received over fifty returned newsletters in one day, prompting him to consider taking matters into his own hands.

Order, Source, and Item Tracking

In addition to his customer files, William also maintains records of his orders, sources, and the books he has available for purchase. As noted above, William has just under 2500 customers. These customers have submitted about 5000 orders involving 12,000 items from about a thousand different sources. Retrieving and refiling folders and cards keeps one of William's assistants busy full time. Currently, William devotes a two-drawer file cabinet to his order records, which are filed sequentially by date in folders marked with the month and year.

William also maintains a folder for each of his sources, including auction houses and individual book dealers who trade in rare books and manuscripts. William maintains data about each source's name, address, phone number, and contact person, as shown in Figure E-2. He also notes each source's specialty, if any; for example, some book dealers trade only in first editions by nineteenth-century American novelists. Each time William purchases an item from a source or acts as a broker between a source and one of his clients, he not only

Source Code	Source Name	Address	Contact
bbc	Ballentine Book Company	4233 S. Charles, Baltimore, MD 21218	Bob Stewart
Ck	Christal S. Kensington	8543 Broton Rd, London SW1P 6QT England	Diane Powell
CNY	Christian, Munson & Wells	50223 5th Ave, New York, NY 10022	Peter Struthers
K	Kanelle & Schwinn	4830 Bielefeld 1 Weiler 9 Germany	Arne Kanelle
P	Sächs Parke Bernet, Inc	31334 Yonkers Ave, New York, NY 10021	Sara Milne
pba	Pacifist Book Auction	1924 Levi St, San Francisco, CA 94133	Steve Michel
pn	Philberts, Son & Nease	101 James Bond St, London W1Y England	Austin Nease
S	Sackesby Italia	Via Pietro Mascagni, 20122 Milan, Italy	Gina Berti
sg	Swain Galleries	104 East 45th St, New York, NY 10010	Cal Swain
wa	Waverlee Book Auctions	4333 Cornell Ave, Baltimore, MD 10814	Betty Waverlee

■ **Figure E-2**

Sample Sources

files a copy of the order, but also records the transaction in the appropriate source and customer files, although sometimes he forgets.

William reads the rare book dealer catalogs religiously to keep abreast of the market. When he finds a particularly good price on a book, he buys the item on speculation, assuming that he'll be able to sell it to one of his clients. Other times, he just notes that particular items are available from particular sources. William maintains a 3-by-5 card file with information about these items. In addition to the author and title, each card lists the place and date of publication, the edition, the type of binding, a brief description of the book's condition (e.g., "original dust jacket," "water damage along top of first several pages"), and any distinguishing features (e.g., "signed by author," "inscribed to President Truman"). In addition, for items he has purchased, William also lists the price he paid for the book; for items that are available for purchase, William notes the asking price of the item. Figure E-3 shows examples of books in William's collection (marked by an asterisk) or on his "good buys" list.

Although William has been very successful, he feels that his burgeoning file drawers are an impediment to business growth. A manual filing system was adequate when he had only a few hundred customers and a few dozen sources. But, now that his reputation has grown, he needs a more efficient way to maintain his records so that he can more effectively serve his customers and market his items. In recent months, he has missed several potential sales opportunities because competing booksellers were able to fill some customer orders more quickly. It seems that these booksellers had a **competitive**

Author	Title	Pub Place	Pub Date	Edition	Binding	Condition	Source	Recent Price
* Anderson	Winesburg, Ohio	NY	1919	1st, 1st iss.		hinge crck'd	P	$80
Faulkner	Absalom, Absalom!	NY	1936	1st		rubbed d/j	bbc	$300
* Faulkner	Absalom, Absalom!	NY	1936	1st	original	Epstein copy	Ck	$1,800
Faulkner	As I Lay Dying	NY	1930	1st	orig cloth	d/j	wa	$275
* Faulkner	Light in August	NY	1932	1st	cloth	chipped	pba	$120
Hawthorne	The Scarlet Letter	NY	1850	1st	orig cloth	Inscr	P	$21,000
* Heinlein	The Green Hills of Earth	Chicago	1951	1st		d/j, edge wear	sg	$120
Heinlein	Stranger in Strange Land	NY	1961	1st		d/j	K	$700
* Hemingway	A Farewell to Arms	NY	1929	Scribner's	orig wraps	worn	sg	$300
Hemingway	A Farewell to Arms	NY	1929	1st	orig cloth	covers spotted	bbc	$1,600
Hemingway	For Whom the Bell Tolls	NY	1940	1st	orig cloth	signed	bbc	$350
Hemingway	For Whom the Bell Tolls	NY	1940	1st	orig cloth	Epstein copy	sg	$4,000
* Hemingway	The Old Man and the Sea	London	1952	1st English		d/j	K	$50
Hemingway	The Old Man and the Sea	NY	1952	1st in Bk		Inscr to WPalmer	sg	$3,400
Hemingway	The Sun Also Rises	NY	1926	1st, 1st iss.		d/j, Epstein copy	sg	$16,000
* Jackson	Haunting of Hill House	NY	1959	1st		d/j	bbc	$100
James	The Portrait of a Lady	London	1881	1st	orig cloth	rubbed, split	S	$1,700
James	Works	NY	1907-	NY Ed.	orig half cloth	worn, discolored	CNY	$3,800
* Kerouac	On the Road	NY	1957	1st		d/j	sg	$80
Kesey	Cuckoo's Nest	NY	1962	1st		d/j, Epstein copy	sg	$500
* Melville	Moby Dick	London	1851	1st	mor gilt	spine worn	CNY	$17,000
* K.A. Porter	Pale Horse, Pale Rider	NY	1939	1st		d/j	wa	$110
* B. Potter	Jemima Puddle-Duck	London	1908	1st	16mo	orig binding	pn	$765
B. Potter	The Tale of Peter Rabbit	London	1901	1st, 1st iss		1/250, Epstein	sg	$50,000
Whitman	Leaves of Grass	Brooklyn	1855	1st, 1st St.	orig cloth	Doheny-Manney	P	$29,000

Note: An asterisk (*) before the item indicates that William owns it.

■ **Figure E-3**

Sample Books

advantage—the ability to produce a product or provide a service more efficiently or more effectively than other firms in the same industry. The competitive advantage of these other booksellers was that they were able to access information to process customer orders more efficiently.

William has considered turning all of his recordkeeping activities over to a service bureau, but, given his less-than-satisfactory experience with the newsletter mailing lists, he has chosen to develop and maintain his own computer-based information system.

Problem Assessment

William hired a business systems consultant, Maria Hernandez, to help him assess his current manual system and develop a computer-based information system. Maria concluded that William needs support for three applications. First, he needs to develop a database to keep track of his customers, sources, items, orders, and customer contacts and to generate mailing labels and periodic ad hoc reports; data from these files would be imported to the word processing application to produce customized form letters. Second, he needs a word processing system that would let him merge customer names, addresses, and information about recent purchases to generate form letters. Third, William needs a desk-top publishing system to produce the customer newsletter. Maria recommended that William follow a **phased development** approach. In this approach, all of the requirements of a system are identified, but the system is divided into subsystems, each subsystem being developed sequentially. Maria suggested that William first develop the database subsystem, then the word processing subsystem, and finally the desk-top publishing subsystem.

Maria helped William select hardware and software that would support all three applications and then began designing the people, procedures, and data components of William's database system. Working with William, she first designed the reports that would help William keep better track of his customers, sources, orders, and books. Figure E-4 shows the Customer Contact Report, which summarizes William's communications with his top three hundred customers over the prior twelve months. Figure E-5 shows a Sales Report, which lists all the sales for a particular period and gives a total sales figure for that period. Figure E-6 shows the Book Inventory Report, which lists information about the books that William owns and gives the total value of his current inventory. Figure E-7 shows the Prospective Sales Report, which relates books to prospective buyers. Maria explained that she would also train William and his assistant to write queries to generate their own reports as needed.

■ **Figure E-4**

Customer Contacts Report

CUSTOMER CONTACTS REPORT
APRIL 30, 1994

- -

TYPE	SUBJECT	NAME	

- -

** Contacts on 03/01/94

L	items on 19C Am list	William	Doyle
L	items on SciFi list	Frank	Charles
L	items on ChildLit list	Marilyn	Baker
L	items on Modern list	Stone	Phillips
L	items on ChildLit list	Steve	Lawrence
L	items on 20C Am list	Kenneth	King
L	items on 19C Am list	James	Stargardt
L	items on Modern list	Jean	Toulouse

** Contacts on 03/05/94

P	Rare Moby Dick in stock	William	Doyle

** Contacts on 03/09/94

P	He called re Pale Horse	Kenneth	King

** Contacts on 03/12/94

P	Peter Rabbit available!	Marilyn	Baker

** Contacts on 03/15/94

P	Competing bid Moby Dick	William	Doyle

** Contacts on 04/25/94

P	Add Jemima to collection?	Marilyn	Baker

L = Letter   P = Phone

■ **Figure E-5**

Sales Report

SALES FOR MARCH – APRIL 1994

DATE	AUTHOR	TITLE	PRICE
** Customer ID is B114			
03/15/94	B. Potter	The Tale of Peter Rabbit	$50000
04/30/94	B. Potter	Jemima Puddle-Duck	765
** Subtotal **			50765
** Customer ID is C067			
04/21/94	Heinlein	Stranger in a Strange Land	700
04/21/94	Heinlein	The Green Hills of Earth	120
** Subtotal **			820
** Customer ID is D322			
03/17/94	Melville	Moby Dick	17000
** Subtotal **			17000
** Customer ID is K142			
03/25/94	K.A. Porter	Pale Horse, Pale Rider	110
** Subtotal **			110
** Customer ID is T183			
03/21/94	Jackson	Haunting of Hill House	100
** Subtotal **			100
*** Total ***			68795

■ **Figure E-6**

Book Inventory Report

BOOK INVENTORY FOR
WILLIAM ELLISON, BOOKSELLER
MARCH 1, 1994

BOOK ID	AUTHOR	TITLE	PRICE
AN10754	Anderson	Winesburg, Ohio	$ 80
FA20543	Faulkner	Absalom, Absalom!	1800
FA39485	Faulkner	Light in August	120
HE00981	Heinlein	The Green Hills of Earth	120
HE00128	Hemingway	A Farewell to Arms	300
HE12002	Hemingway	The Old Man and the Sea	50
JA33333	Jackson	Haunting of Hill House	100
KE00876	Kerouac	On the Road	80
ME00988	Melville	Moby Dick	17000
PO99923	K.A. Porter	Pale Horse, Pale Rider	110
PO00222	B. Potter	Jemima Puddle-Duck	765
*** Total ***			
			20525

■ **Figure E-7**

Prospective Sales Report

PROSPECTIVE SALES REPORT

FIRST NAME	LAST NAME	PHONE NUMBER
** Interest is 19th Cent American		
William	Doyle	(216) 779-5050
James	Stargardt	049-4033-69 90 22
** Interest is 20th Cent American		
Kenneth	King	061-0347-88 42 17
Jean	Toulouse	033-9901-76 89 71
** Interest is Children's Lit		
Marilyn	Baker	011-0522-75 88 99
Steve	Lawrence	011-7033-90 75 22
** Interest is Modern		
Stone	Phillips	044-0311-87 09 66
** Interest is Science Fiction		
Frank	Charles	(213) 757-8800

■ QUESTIONS AND EXERCISES

■ **Step I: Problem Analysis** In order to develop an information system to automate William's existing record-keeping processes and to support additional processes, you first need to understand his current system and identify its functions and inadequacies. In this step, you will identify the **user requirements** of William's database subsystem.

1. What are William's business **objectives** in developing this subsystem?

2. What business functions does William's current manual record-keeping system support? How well does his system support these functions?

3. What additional functions does William expect his new database subsystem to support?

4. What are the input, processing, output, and storage requirements of the database subsystem?

■ **Step II: Database Design**   Assume that William has acquired the hardware to support his database system. Assume also that he has purchased a DBMS that will allow him to store data as tables. The first step in designing a database is to build a model of the data it will contain. (See Appendix DB1 for information about data modeling.) The principles of good database design dictate that each table should contain data about only one entity or object (e.g., a generic person, place, thing, or event). An **entity** is a person, place, thing, or event about which data is maintained. For example, in this case, Source is an entity; each particular source, for example, Swain Galleries, is an instance of an entity: a real-world manifestation of the entity Source.

1. Review the case and, more specifically, the outputs that William's system will need to generate. List the entities represented by the data in these reports.

2. An **attribute** is a characteristic or property of an entity; for example, some of the attributes of the Source entity are its code, name, address, and contact person. A **key identifier** is an attribute that uniquely identifies each instance of an entity. The key identifier of the Source entity can be either its name (assuming no two names are the same) or its code. Thus, the Source entity as we've defined it so far can be modeled as

SOURCE

SourceCode	SourceName	SourceAddress	SourceContact

Create a similar representation for each of the entities you identified in Exercise 1; list each entity's attributes, and underline the attribute that will serve as the entity's key identifier.

3. In a relational database, each entity is represented as a table. The columns of the table contain attributes of the entity; each row represents an instance of an entity, that is, all the data maintained about it. For example,

SOURCE

SourceCode	SourceName	SourceAddress	SourceContact
sg	Swain Galleries	104 E. 45th St New York NY 10010	Cal Swain
S	Sackesby Italia	Via Pietro Mascagni, 20122, Milan, Italy	Gina Berti

Any time two entities are related to each other, the key identifier of one is placed in the table of the other. For example, the entities Source and Book are related in that a Source can provide many Books and each Book is provided by one Source. Each cell (the intersection of a row and a column) in a table can contain *only one* data value. Thus, we can't establish a relationship between the two tables by placing Book's key identifier in the Source table because each Source will provide many Books. Instead, we place the key identifier of Source in the Book table because each Book is provided by *one and only one* Source:

BOOK

BookID	BookAuthor	...	SourceCode

Having established a link between the Book and Source tables, we will be able to produce reports that contain data from both tables. See Appendix DB1 for more information about data modeling.

Using these ideas, modify your entities as necessary.

4. Review the user requirements that you defined in Step I. As currently defined, will your database design support all the requirements? For example, will you be able to print mailing labels and use a customer's first name and the title of a recent purchase in a letter? Will your design of the customer and source phone numbers support international numbers? If necessary, modify your entities to meet the user requirements.

5. Now that you have identified the tables in the database, you need to describe the **physical file structure** of each table by listing the fields for each file and identifying their field type (e.g., character, numeric, date) and field width.

■ **Step III: Database Implementation** You're now ready to begin implementing the database. Use your chosen relational DBMS to perform the exercises below.

1. Following the physical design you outlined in Step II, create and save the file structure for each entity. Then enter and save 10–15 records for each file, using the data provided in the case figures as a starting point. Print a listing of each file's contents.

2. Print the Book Inventory Report using a report format file so that you can replicate Maria's report layout.

3. Print the Prospective Sales Report using a report format file so that you can replicate Maria's report layout.

4. Print the Customer Contact Report.
   a. Begin by identifying the files that must be accessed to generate this report.

   b. The Customer Contact Report will be generated on a regular basis. Therefore, it makes sense to create a database view for this report.

   c. After you have created the Customer Contact database view, create and save a report format file so that you can replicate Maria's report layout.

5. Print the Sales Report.
   a. Begin by identifying the file(s) that must be accessed to generate this report.

b. The Sales Report will be generated on a regular basis. Therefore, it makes sense to create a database view for this report.

c. After you have created the Sales Report database view, create and save a report format file so that you can replicate Maria's report layout.

6. William wants to rescue his mailing list from the service bureau. Create a **label format file** so that William can generate his own mailing labels.

7. William also needs to be able to generate ad hoc reports. Query the appropriate files to generate each of the following reports:
   a. As William was reading a book dealer's catalog that arrived in the mail today, he came across an exceptionally good price on a hard-to-find edition of a Henry James novel. Query the client file to print the name and phone number of all customers who have a special interest in 19th Century American writers so that William can call to alert these book collectors of a special find.

   b. A book collector has just called and wants to know about any books by William Faulkner available for purchase. Query the book file to print all the information about books written by Faulkner.

8. Verify that the reports generated in 2–7 above are correct by comparing your file contents listings to each report.

■ **Step IV: Post-Implementation Review** Having developed your database system, you now need to evaluate how well it satisfies user requirements and how it will help William compete more effectively.

1. Review the user requirements you identified in Step I. How well does the database subsystem meet these requirements?

2. Review the business objectives you identified in Step I. Does your database subsystem help William achieve these objectives?

3. One of the factors that motivated William to invest the time and money required to develop this system was that he was losing customers and sales to competing book dealers. In other words, he felt that his manual filing system was an obstacle to his business growth and competitiveness.

   Information systems serve three roles in helping a firm address the competitive forces in its industry: they (a) improve operational efficiency, (b) promote business innovation, and (c) build strategic information resources. **Operational efficiency** describes how a firm can cut costs, speed up its transactions, and improve quality using information technology. **Business innovation** involves using information technology to produce new products or services or to redesign existing processes. A **strategic information resource** provides information to support a firm's marketing and strategic planning activities.

   Analyze how William's new database system serves these three roles.

Case 5:
To Automate or Not to Automate: A Cost-Benefit Analysis for EPT

Learning Objectives

The purposes of this case are to analyze the cost feasibility of an in-house trading support system and to investigate the appropriateness of an information system that could potentially pose a threat to an organization's existence. Specifically, in this case you will

1. Describe the current business operations of a commodities trading firm.
2. Describe the potential features and functions of an information system that supports commodities trading.
3. Use a spreadsheet to investigate the costs and benefits of such an information system.
4. Assess the risks of an information system that could possibly eliminate the market for the company that spawned it.

■ Spreadsheet Skills Required

Basic

1. Format a worksheet by entering headings and labels and specifying column width and cell type/format.
2. Write formulas to sum a range of cells.
3. Copy formulas using **absolute and relative cell references.**

Advanced

4. Create and print graphs.
5. Perform What if . . . ? analyses by modifying the worksheet.

We assume that students possess the basic skills listed above. The advanced skill—creating and printing graphs—is discussed in Appendix SS2.

Background

Al Maloney has been a produce trader for thirty-five years. He buys from produce growers and sells to packaged food companies. Most of his buyers are very large companies that require tens or hundreds of thousands of pounds of different types of fruits and vegetables each week.

Al's chief assets are his relationships with several hundred growers and dozens of buyers. From years of experience, he knows the personalities, habits, tendencies, and the pressures that bear upon both groups of people. This knowledge and these contacts are the key to his business success.

The following excerpts from typical telephone conversations give a sense of Al's business:

"Harry, this is Al. How are you? Yeah, really? Fine. My kids are fine too. Thanks. Say, Harry, I've got ten thousand pounds of Queen Anne cherries I could deliver by Friday. Well, for a long-standing customer like you, Harry, the price is eight and a half. . . . Well, OK, you know your business. . . . Blueberries? What grade? You must be dreaming, Harry. You know you can't find Grade A blues this time of year. No way! I'll look around a bit, but you're kidding yourself."

"Yeah, Mario, how you doing? Been out in your new boat? Kids waterskiing yet? I'll bet so. Mario, I've got some Queen Anne cherries I could deliver. . . . 10,000 pounds. . . . Well, Mario, for as long as we've known each other, I could let you have them for eight and a quarter. . . . How about Friday? OK. Good to talk to you."

"Hello, Sammy. What have you been up to lately? Been up to the city? You crazy guy. No, Sammy, I'm too old for that. Cherries? What price? Sammy, I've got plenty of cherries, especially at that price. I might be interested in some blues, though. Grade A. . . . B's? You only got B's? How come nobody grows quality anymore, Sammy? Are those good B or rotten B? Oh, come on, you and I been round the block a few times. . . . "

"Good morning, Jonathan. . . . Warm, unseasonably warm, in fact. . . . Well, thank you. Actually, this morning, Jonathan, I'm purchasing Grade AA blueberries. No? That's a shame. I wish more growers would put an emphasis on quality. Grade A? Well, I don't know. How many pounds? Hmmm. I would prefer Grade AA. What would be the price? . . . Jonathan, my buyer is very particular. I'm not certain that he'd accept Grade A, and that price is too high. They might accept A's at twelve and a half. . . . Oh, I think they'd take the whole lot. All right, Jonathan, let's say twelve and three-quarters."

"Harry, this is your lucky day! I found the blues. Grade A, tops. I can get you 70,000 pounds, Monday delivery in Minneapolis. . . . Fifteen. . . .

Sorry, Harry, that's the price, fifteen. Take it or leave it. . . . OK, they're comin' your way. Boy, are you lucky!"

Al understands how time impacts both growers and buyers and influences the prices they are willing to accept. The growers need to sell while their crops are fresh and marketable. Buyers, on the other hand, need raw produce to meet production work schedules. Growers fear rotten, unsold crops, and buyers fear idle production lines. Al works the line between the growers and the buyers, and he charges a 15 to 20 percent markup for his services.

Emerson Produce Traders consists of a group of eight traders and an office manager/accountant. Al and two other traders own the group. The other five traders work for a salary plus a commission on the sales they make.

Emerson Produce Traders has been operating for twenty-two years. The business has been run with little change in operations over that period. Recently, however, one of the new traders, Mike Sharnsby, a recent business school graduate, has introduced the notion of improving business processes using information technology.

A Proposed Commodities Trading Information System

"Look, Al," said Mike, "here's how it would work. Each buyer would have a computer that's connected to a common data source, called a database. The database would keep records of who bought what and when they bought it and also of what buyers and sellers currently want.

"Take an example. Suppose you find someone who wants twenty thousand pounds of white seedless grapes. You would access your computer to see if there was any grower selling grapes, and if so, you'd call him or whatever. If not, then you'd put the name of your buyer and what he wanted in the database. When another trader finds a grower with grapes, he'd contact your customer."

"Geez, kid, that's crazy! Why would we want to do that? First, I don't want nobody calling my customers—buyers or sellers. Second, if I'm in a pinch, for either a grower or a buyer, I write it on the trading board over there, like you do, or at least, like you should. What would I need a computer for?"

Al was pointing at a large white board that covered three sides of the trading room. The phrase "Wanted to Buy" was written on the top of one board. The phrase "Wanted to Sell" was written on top of a second board. By custom, whenever a trader had a grower who was in a pinch to sell a crop, the trader would describe the goods on the "Wanted to Sell" board. Similarly, the needs of buyers who were in a bind were written at the top of the "Wanted to Buy" board. The traders listed their initials and a description of the goods needed on the public board. The names of the growers or buyers were held back so that each trader could be sure that he was included in the deal.

"Al, here's another thought. We could develop the system so that you would be sure to be involved in all of your deals. We could follow the same process as you do now with the trading board, but do it on the computer."

"Yeah, we could. But why? What's wrong with the trading board?"

"Well, for one, there's no history. An information system would keep track of past deals. The traders could use it to remind themselves who bought and sold what goods at what times. Wouldn't you like to know all of the trades you made last year at this time? So you could call some of the same growers and buyers?"

"Kid, I know what deals I did last year, and the year before that, and the year before that. Knowing all of that is what I do, that's what I'm paid for. I don't need no computer to tell me that."

"But Al, what about sending letters to customers, summarizing their trading activity, reminding them of us, sort of a marketing-oriented service."

"I tell you, kid, I just don't see it. Things are fine as they are. Spend your time learning the produce business. That's what we hired you for."

An Electronic Market

Mike was not at all satisfied by his conversation with Al. While he thought the trading business was interesting and his job would pay a more than adequate living, something bothered him about Al's attitude.

During idle moments and in his spare time, Mike continued to think about the advantages of an electronic commodities trading system to facilitate the traders' activities. "Hey," he thought to himself, "we could let growers and buyers dial into our system. They could pay a fee for the right to use our data." Mike developed this idea further in his own mind and then went back and described it to Al.

"Kid, you gotta be crazy! You're nuts. You know what that would do?"

"Well, it would make it a lot easier for our customers, for one."

"No, pal, no. It would put us out of business! That's what. With that system, what would our customers need us for? Huh? Think about it. They pay me my commission because I know where to go to find or sell what they want. If they could do it for themselves, I'm out of business."

"But, Al, we could charge a fee."

"Yeah. How much? Fifty cents a peek? Come on, we'll never make any money doing that. We'd just be giving our business away with a computer."

"Al, somebody's gonna do it. Think about it. If it can be done, and if you don't do it, somebody will."

Al's eyes narrowed and he looked hard at Mike.

"Kid, pick up your check. Get outta here! Out of here! We don't need no snot-nosed college kid telling us how to run our business. We been doing it a long time."

"Al, that's not what I meant. I don't mean I'm gonna do it. But somebody else will!"

"I'm feeling real bad right now, kid, so just get outta here. Clean out your desk and go! I'll send you your check. Just get gone! Now!"

Further Steps

Mike is the kind of person who, once he bites into an idea, just can't let go of it. And his usual tenacity was only strengthened by Al's response to his idea of developing a commodities trading system. During the days following his dismissal from Emerson Produce Traders, he talked with business systems consultants and scoured books and trade journals to find support for his claim that "If it can be done, and if you don't do it, somebody will." He wanted to go back to Al with proof that a commodities trading system was not only feasible but also inevitable.

Mike visited a business systems consultant and described Emerson's situation, without mentioning the company by name. The consultant compared Emerson's business processes to those of a stock brokerage house and explained how most stocks today are traded electronically, if not directly between the stockholder (Emerson's growers) and stock buyer (Emerson's produce buyers), then almost always among stock brokers on the exchange. The consultant also noted that information technology in the financial markets had first been used in-house. Only after the systems were proven and their uses fully understood did a few companies begin letting clients log on to a network to post buys and sells themselves.

Mike understood the wisdom of starting in-house and proving the soundness of the system before opening it to buyer and grower access. Compiling the information gathered from his reading and conversations, Mike outlined the hardware and software requirements of an in-house trading support system. Emerson Produce Traders could develop a local area network (LAN) using nine PCs (one for each trader and one for the office manager/accountant) as the nodes and a super PC as a server. They could use a LAN operating system such as Microsoft's LAN MANAGER and a server DBMS such as SQL Server with client DBMS products such as DataEase or Paradox. All of the PCs would also be networked to a laser printer. . . .

■ QUESTIONS AND EXERCISES

■ **Step I: Problem Analysis**   Mike has proposed two types of information systems: an in-house trading support system to be used only by the traders, and an electronic commodities market to be used directly by growers and buyers. In these exercises, we will focus on the former, the in-house trading support system, and analyze its costs and benefits.

1. Describe the current business operations of Emerson Produce Traders. What information is needed? How is it obtained?

2. List, in general terms, the advantages and disadvantages of developing an in-house trading support system. How would you determine whether such a system should be developed?

3. Describe the characteristics of one potential system alternative. Mike has provided a start for you by describing some hardware and software alternatives. Elaborate on Mike's system description, describing the necessary hardware, software, data, procedures, and personnel components.

4. Evaluate the way that Mike broached the idea of an in-house trading support system to Al. Think in terms of the kind of person Al is. How might Mike have proceeded differently to avoid antagonizing Al?

Your task in this exercise is to project—over a five-year period—the costs and benefits of the system you described in Exercise 3 above. Early on, when an organization is just beginning to consider developing an information system, it's important to determine the system's **cost feasibility.** Cost feasibility addresses the question, "Is an information system within the appropriate realm of cost?" In other words, are the anticipated benefits to be derived from the system equal to or greater than its expected costs? Questions 5–7 below ask you to consider these costs and benefits. In this analysis, you don't need to have exact figures, just ballpark estimates of the system's likely costs and benefits.

5. What would be the costs of developing and operating this system? Consider both the initial **development costs** (including hiring someone to design and implement the system and purchasing hardware, software, etc.) and the **production costs** of operating and maintaining the system (including additional labor costs, planned hardware and software upgrades, etc.).

6. What **tangible benefits** could Emerson gain by implementing this system? Tangible benefits are those that can be readily quantified. For example, reduced labor costs, reduced costs per transaction, increased transactions per day, new sources of income made possible by the system, and so on. Estimate the dollar value of each of these benefits.

7. What **intangible benefits** could Emerson gain by implementing this system? Intangible benefits are those that are not readily quantified. For example, improved employee morale, improved business reputation, better customer service, and so on.

   Where possible, try to quantify these intangible benefits. For example, improved business reputation and better customer service may mean more customers and more repeat business, respectively. Given that Al's commission on the blueberries sale was $1500, a system that netted even one more sale a week would yield an annual benefit of $78,000!

■ **Step II: Worksheet Design**   A spreadsheet is a very useful tool for performing cost-benefit analysis. A spreadsheet not only helps you format your analysis report and perform calculations; it also allows you to manipulate your estimates of costs and benefits to see how sensitive the cost feasibility of the system is to variations in these estimates. In this exercise, you will design and implement a worksheet to analyze the costs and benefits of the system you described in Exercise 3 above.

You've already begun the first two steps in a cost-benefit analysis: estimating the costs and estimating the benefits. The third step is to calculate the **payback point:** the time required to accumulate enough benefit dollars to "pay back" the cost dollars. Where a system has no production costs and stable benefits (that is, the dollar value of the benefits does not vary from one year to the next), one can use a simple formula to calculate the payback point:

Development costs / Benefits per year = Years to payback

For example, if a system costs $100,000 to develop, has no production costs, and stable benefits of $25,000 per year, the payback point is 4 years.

Unfortunately, this simple formula does not fit most systems; most systems do incur production costs, and their benefits do vary over time. In these situations, one must use a table that accumulates costs and benefits to calculate the payback point. Figure P-1 shows an excerpt of a worksheet table used to perform these calculations. Please note that, in this table, development

■ Figure P-1

Assumptions

	Year 1
Annual Increase/Decrease in Prod	10%
Annual Increase/Decrease in Bene	10%
COSTS	
Development Costs	
Hardware	$50,000
Software	$7,500
Consultant	$20,000
Training	$20,000
Total Development Costs	$97,500
Production Costs	
Supplies	$1,200
Network Support Personnel	$18,000
Maintenance/Upgrades	$2,500
Other costs?	
Annual Production Costs	$21,700
Accumulated Costs	$119,200
BENEFITS	
Productivity	$78,000
Other benefits?	
Accumulated Benefits	$78,000
NET FOR YEAR	($41,200)

costs have been added to Year 1 production costs. Some people prefer to include a Year 0 to indicate the development time and costs. That approach requires an explanation of what "Year 0" is; our approach requires an explanation that "development costs have been added to Year 1 production costs." Either way, you should understand that Year 1 begins the day that the system is put into use and that development costs for Years 2–5 are zero.

In our example analysis, we have estimated benefits by assuming that the system will increase productivity by one trade per week. This is a very conservative estimate, but, considering that Al made $1500 on his blueberry sale, even one additional trade yields a high payoff. The development costs are ballpark figures, using the high end of a $2000–$5000 per node estimate for network hardware (PCs, cabling, etc.). For production costs, we have estimated about $100 per month for supplies and about $1500 per month for a part-time network support person. All of these figures are "guesstimates"; by doing some research, you can probably come up with better figures.

Your job is to complete the design of the example worksheet by answering the following questions.

1. Considering only the costs and benefits for Year 1, what calculations are needed to determine the total costs, total benefits, and net gain or loss for the first year?

2. Write a formula to compute the accumulated net gain or loss for Years 2–5.

3. Assume that we anticipate a 10 percent annual increase in production costs and benefits for Years 2–5. Assume also that we want to be able to manipulate this estimate to determine the effect of various increases or decreases in costs and benefits. For example, we may want to see what happens to the payback point if we estimate a 15 percent increase in production costs and no increase in benefits. To perform this kind of analysis, you need to include assumption input cells as shown in Figure P-1. How will you have to design your worksheet and incorporate formulas to support this kind of analysis?

4. Knowing how skeptical Al is about the value of information systems for his business, you need to build flexibility into your worksheet so that you can easily manipulate static data about the initial development and production costs and benefits. Plan to include sensitivity factors—one for costs and one for benefits—in your assumptions/input data section so that you can model the effects of higher than expected initial costs and/or benefits in your worksheet. These are not shown in Figure P-1; you will need to determine how best to incorporate these requirements.

5. Review Figure P-1 to design the rest of the worksheet. Then determine appropriate column widths, cell types, and cell formats for your worksheet.

6. In addition to providing a table such as the one shown in Figure P-1, you may also want to use a graph to illustrate the costs, benefits, and payback point. What kind of graph would be appropriate to illustrate these relationships?

■ **Step III: Worksheet Implementation**   As you construct your worksheet, you will write a number of formulas that reference cell locations. You will need to use a combination of absolute cell references and relative cell references in these formulas. In most spreadsheet products, an **absolute cell reference** includes a dollar sign before the column and row numbers, e.g., A25; an absolute cell reference always refers to the same cell, even if the formula is copied to another location. In your formulas, you will need to use absolute cell references to refer to cells that contain, for example, your estimates of annual increase/decrease in production costs and benefits.

A **relative cell reference** is represented simply by the column letter and row number, for example, as A25. A relative cell reference is one that is interpreted as a location relative to the current cell. For example, assume the formula @sum(A20.A24) is located in cell A25. The spreadsheet interprets this formula as "sum the contents of the five cells directly above the current cell and place the result in the current cell." Thus, when you copy this formula to cell B25, the formula stored in B25 is @sum(B20.B24). You will need to use relative cell references when you copy cells that contain formulas.

1. Begin constructing your worksheet by first laying out two sections: one for input data and another for calculations and output. Then enter column headings, set column widths and formats, etc. Include appropriate labels and input cells for the assumptions about annual increase/decrease in production costs and benefits. Then enter the individual cost and benefit estimates in your input data section.

2. Write formulas in the appropriate cells of your calculations/output section to compute the total costs, total benefits, and net gain/loss for Year 1.

3. Write formulas in the appropriate cells to compute the individual cost and benefit figures for Year 2. Copy these formulas to the appropriate cells for Years 3–5.

4. Copy the formulas for total costs and total benefits for Year 1 to the appropriate cells for Years 2–5.

5. In the cell for Year 2 net gain/loss, write a formula to calculate the accumulated net/gain loss. Then copy this formula to the appropriate cells for Years 3–5.

6. Print your worksheet. What is the payback point for the in-house trading support system?

7. Generate and print a graph to illustrate the costs, benefits, and payback point.

8. Conduct a What if…? analysis. Manipulate your estimates of costs and benefits to examine the effect on payback point. For example, what happens if development costs are 20 percent higher or lower? If your initial estimate of benefits is off by 25 percent? If annual production costs increase 15 percent in Years 2–5? Manipulate these assumptions however you think appropriate, noting their effects on payback so that you can use them to answer some of the Post-Implementation Review questions.

■ **Step IV: Post-Implementation Review**

1. Given your analysis of the costs and benefits of the in-house trading
    support system, should Al develop the system? What other factors
    need to be considered in making this decision?

2. Referring to the manipulations you performed in Exercise 8 above,
    discuss the sensitivity of payback to changes in costs or benefits. For
    example, does even a small increase in cost estimates seriously affect
    the payback point? How confident are you in your recommendation to
    Al about developing the system, given your cost-benefit analysis?

3. How do you think Al would have responded if Mike had performed
    a cost-benefit analysis and presented the results to Al at the time that
    he first brought up the idea of an in-house trading support system?

4. Write a memo in which you discuss the features, costs, and benefits
    of an in-house trading support system and recommend that Al
    develop/not develop the system. Refer to your worksheet and graph
    where appropriate, and indicate how confident you are in your
    analysis. Discuss any management or human issues that would cause
    you to recommend that Al act on factors other than financial costs
    and benefits.

Shift your focus for the following questions, and consider the electronic commodities market that Mike described.

5. The primary difference between the in-house trading support system and the electronic commodities market can be summarized using the words of Michael Hammer, a specialist in business process reengineering: The in-house system just "paves the cowpaths," whereas the electronic commodities market revolutionizes the way trades are made. More and more, businesses today are discovering that significant improvements in productivity require them to rethink fundamental business processes; just doing business the old way isn't good enough in today's highly competitive business environment.

    Considering these comments, is Mike right when he says, "If it can be done and you don't do it, somebody will"?

6. This system would be accessed by both growers and buyers. Is Al right? Does such a system put Emerson out of business? Why or why not?

7. As noted, Al made $1500 on the blueberry sales transaction. Would customers be willing to pay that much if they arranged the trade themselves using the electronic commodities market? If not, does that fact make the electronic commodities market infeasible due to cost? Why or why not?

8. How would you have to modify the in-house trading support system to develop an electronic commodities market? Describe the additional features required.

9. Al clearly tailors his approach and even his conversational style to his customers, thus personalizing his service. This personal style is part of Al's product, and it would be lost in an electronic commodities market. How important do you think this loss would be to the customers?

Case 6:
An Inventory Management System for JKC

Part A:

Plant Inventory Database

Learning Objectives

The purpose of this case is to demonstrate how a business can improve its efficiency and effectiveness by implementing a database to manage its inventory. Specifically, in this case you will:

1. Define the problem to be solved by specifying **user requirements.**
2. Use a DBMS to develop an inventory database and generate reports.
3. Examine the business benefits of this inventory management system.

■ Database Skills Required

Basic

1. Create file structures.
2. Enter records.
3. Write queries using single and **compound conditions.**
4. **Sort** a file on a sort key.
5. **Link files** to generate a report.

Advanced

6. Create and use a database **view file** to generate a report.
7. Create and use a **report format** file to generate a report.

We assume that students already possess all the basic database skills listed above. The advanced skills 6 and 7 are discussed in Appendices DB2 and DB3, respectively.

Background

Jenson-Kehrwald Company (JKC) is a partnership that designs and develops interior landscapes for hotels, restaurants, condominiums, and large private estates. In their designs, they use a mixture of commonly available plants, flowers, and shrubs, and imported rare and exotic plants, pottery, and other materials. JKC employs twenty-five people and has gross sales of $3.6 million with a before-tax profit of $648,000. Elizabeth Jenson and Chip Kehrwald own the partnership equally. Elizabeth, a designer, manages the artistic side of the business—including not only supervising the design activity, but also job production and the selection of vendors. Chip is the general manager who manages the inventory and supervises the sales and financial activities.

The Order Process

One of the JKC salespeople calls upon a customer and identifies an opportunity. Once the salespeople identify a real prospect, they introduce one or more of JKC's six designers to the customer. The designers meet with the customer, determine the customer's needs, and then develop a design, including formal sketches and blueprints. The designers also prepare a written bid that contains a general description of the project, a list of plants and materials, and a detailed listing of both material and labor costs. The design is reviewed with the customer, adjusted as needed, and then approved (or rejected). If approved, the project is turned over to the Production Department for implementation. Accounts Receivable then follows up for payment.

Usually, customers are slow to approve the design, but, once they do approve it, they want almost immediate implementation. Because JKC's procurement process is very slow, the designers have learned to work only with plants and materials that are in inventory or that will very soon be in inventory. Except for very large and specialized jobs, the designers do not have the luxury of selecting plants that are not already on order or in inventory.

Inventory Management

One of the **critical success factors** for JKC is inventory management. They must have appropriate plants available when needed; however, because their inventory is expensive to maintain, they do not want more inventory than necessary. But with **order lead time** averaging four weeks, they need to maintain sufficient stock to carry them until the ordered items are delivered.

The Design Group keeps inventory records to facilitate the effective use of inventory. Specifically, for each plant type, they maintain data about the plant type, size, average net cost, list price, quantity on hand, and quantity on order.

An excerpt of this inventory data is shown in Table 1. This inventory data is maintained in a master notebook by the Design Group's administrative assistant, Anne Rogers. Each day, Anne updates the quantity-on-hand (QOH) and quantity-on-order (QOO) numbers and makes a copy of the master record for each designer. The designers work against the data on these copies in deciding which plants to include in their designs. At the end of each day, the designers give Anne a list of the plants they have used; Anne then subtracts these items from the QOH records. Also, each day, Anne checks with Chip to update QOO data. She also receives delivery data from the Greenhousing Department and updates QOH totals accordingly.

There are a number of problems with this arrangement. For one, designers work simultaneously, and sometimes they unknowingly take the same last items from inventory. They try to coordinate their activities to prevent this, but sometimes it is not possible. Another problem concerns verifying physical inventory. Currently, Anne subtracts an item from the quantity-on-hand total as soon as a designer uses that item in a design. However, the plant remains in

■ Table 1	Plant Type	Size	AveNet$	List$	QOH	QOO
Sample Inventory Data	laccospadix australasica palm	15 gal	$450.00	$751.00	3	0
	arenga pinnata palm	15 gal	$310.00	$517.00	4	0
	chamaedorea falcifera palm	15 gal	$300.00	$501.00	0	2
	ceratozamia molongo palm	14 in	$240.00	$400.00	2	4
	arecastum coco plumosa	15 gal	$275.00	$459.00	11	0
	caryota mitis	7 gal	$140.00	$233.00	14	0
	phoenix robellini	14 in	$105.00	$175.00	8	6
	chamaedorea "bamboo"	14 in	$110.00	$183.00	5	2
	raphis palm	14 in	$350.00	$584.00	7	6
	spath deneve	14 in	$ 90.00	$150.00	15	0
	corynocarpus leav	16 in	$130.00	$217.00	12	5
	ti character	10 gal	$155.00	$258.00	11	0
	red ti character	7 gal	$140.00	$233.00	0	10
	green ti	7 gal	$140.00	$233.00	8	6
	j c compacta	3 gal	$ 55.00	$ 91.00	17	1
	green ti	5 gal	$ 92.00	$153.00	11	0
	raphis palm	3 gal	$180.00	$300.00	12	1
	ficus green gem	14 in	$ 90.00	$150.00	7	8
	ficus green gem	17 in	$240.00	$400.00	6	3
	marginata	2 gal	$ 45.00	$ 75.00	16	0

physical inventory until it is actually removed by Production workers. Overseeing physical inventory is the responsibility of the Greenhousing Department, which performs all shipping and receiving tasks as well as caring for the plants in inventory. The Greenhouse clerk, Bob Edwards, agrees with Anne that the difference between the "paper" inventory and the physical inventory creates several problems.

First, if a design is changed to eliminate plants, these plants should be placed back in inventory; that is, Anne should add them back into the QOH total. Sometimes designers forget to tell Anne about these changes. As a result, the physical inventory is usually larger than the records show. Second, although Anne updates her "paper" inventory each time a shipment of plants arrives and each time a designer includes a plant in a bid, she does not keep track of the stock items actually being removed from physical inventory. Thus, it is possible for plants to "disappear" from the greenhouse. Unfortunately, there is no easy way to detect this disappearance—a major concern for the Greenhouse clerk—because Anne has no record of the actual quantity of each plant type that is supposed to be in physical inventory at any given time.

Another problem with the current inventory system is that designers would like to be able to "reserve" plants on order for use in their designs. Anne has considered adding two columns to her master notebook inventory sheet: one column would give the quantity of items in-stock and on-bid, and the other column would give the quantity of items on-order and on-bid. Thus, instead of subtracting in-stock items from the QOH when a designer uses them, Anne would add them to the quantity in-stock and on-bid. A designer would know how many items were available by subtracting the quantity on-bid from the quantity on-hand. Similar procedures would need to be instituted for maintaining data about quantity on-order and on-bid.

The primary advantages of these procedural changes would be that the designers can reserve plants on order and that Anne can work with the Greenhouse clerk to keep a more accurate record of physical inventory.

Increasing Competition

A major concern for JKC is competition. In recent years, a number of similar firms have begun operation, and business that at one time was easy to obtain has now become very competitive. Due to competitive pressure, JKC is increasingly required to reduce its prices. While on the one hand, Elizabeth and Chip strive to provide the best and not necessarily the cheapest product, on the other hand, they cannot entirely ignore price levels set by their competition. To retain profitability in this environment, JKC must be as efficient as possible in all aspects of its business. This means buying at a low price and passing on those savings to their customers. This goal has been difficult to achieve because the plant inventory data does not indicate the actual purchase cost of each item. It also means that JKC needs to minimize the costs of ordering and maintaining its inventory. As shown in Table 2, Chip maintains data about each plant type's preferred and back-up suppliers with their order lead times (shown in parentheses beside supplier name) and annual sales. However, he currently uses this data only to select a supplier for each plant type when he places an order.

Action Taken So Far

Elizabeth and Chip met with Eric Diehl, a business systems consultant, to discuss their inventory management problems. In addition to the problems outlined above, Eric determined that JKC was also having trouble managing its inventory costs. JKC was selling some of its plants at an incorrect price because the markup was based on the generic purchase cost of a plant type. As part of his management duties, Chip needs to be able to keep track of the actual cost of

■ Table 2	DESC	Size	Sales/Yr	Supplier1	Supplier2
Suppliers, Lead Times, and Sales for Each Plant Type	laccospadix australasica palm	15 gal	50	Palms(4)	Lunds(5)
	arenga pinnata palm	15 gal	80	GPC(2)	Greens(3)
	chamaedorea falcifera palm	15 gal	35	Palms(4)	Lunds(5)
	ceratozamia molongo palm	14"	85	Palms(4)	Lunds(5)
	arecastum coco plumosa	15 gal	135	Greens(3)	GPC(2)
	caryota mitis	7 gal	170	Olsen(3)	Greens(3)
	phoenix robellini	14"	155	Lunds(5)	Greens(3)
	chamaedorea "bamboo"	14"	115	China(8)	Palms(9)
	raphis palm	14"	135	Palms(4)	Lunds(5)
	spath deneve	14"	175	Greens(3)	GPC(2)
	corynocarpus leav	16"	200	Greens(3)	GPC(2)
	ti character	10 gal	120	TisRUs(7)	Olsen(9)
	red ti character	7 gal	135	TisRUs(7)	Olsen(9)
	green ti	7 gal	180	TisRUs(7)	Olsen(9)
	j c compacta	3 gal	250	GPC(2)	Lunds(5)
	green ti	5 gal	160	TisRUs(7)	Olsen(9)
	raphis palm	3 gal	150	Palms(4)	Lunds(5)
	ficus green gem	14"	200	Figs(4)	Lunds(5)
	ficus green gem	17"	100	Figs(4)	Lunds(5)
	marginata	2 gal	230	GPC(2)	Greens(3)

each plant in inventory to prepare inventory tax reports and to determine an appropriate list price for each plant (usually a 67% markup over net cost). JKC was maintaining cost data on each plant type (e.g., that the cost of a 7-gallon green ti averaged $140). But it needed to maintain this data about each particular plant (e.g., that the cost of the 7-gallon green ti #33 was $152). By so doing, JKC would know the actual cost of each item in inventory and would be able to set its list price accordingly.

Initially, Eric recommended that JKC develop an integrated system that would employ a network of 10 workstations to computerize its bid generation, purchasing, and inventory processes. Although Elizabeth and Chip recognized the advantages of such an integrated system, they decided to "start small"— that is, they opted to develop a network of two computers (one in Anne's office and one in Chip's) to maintain data about plant inventory. Because JKC was currently a "computer free zone," Elizabeth and Chip felt that they needed to make the move to automation in small steps. If this rudimentary system worked out, then they would consider phasing in the integrated system Eric had recommended.

Anne had completed several MIS courses as an evening student at Cal State. She felt that, if Eric installed the hardware and software, she could create the database using a popular microcomputer-based DBMS. Eric outlined a general plan for developing a Plant Inventory Management System (PIMS) for JKC. As a first step, Anne would develop an inventory database listing relevant information about all plant types and individual plant items.

Anne would maintain all data about inventory status from copies of (1) the designers' bids, (2) Chip's purchase orders, (3) Greenhousing's receiving reports, and (4) Production's work orders (listing items removed from inventory). Anne would also generate daily inventory status reports for the designers, weekly reports of expected shipments and periodic physical inventory verification reports for Greenhousing, and low inventory reports for Chip, in addition to any ad-hoc reports required.

■ QUESTIONS AND EXERCISES

In these questions and exercises, you will analyze the problems facing JKC and then design solutions to these problems and implement components of the Plant Inventory Management System (PIMS) using a DBMS. Eric Diehl has recommended that JKC implement a plant inventory database to alleviate its inventory management problems. Your job is to design and implement a database that will maintain data about each plant type (e.g., description, size) and each plant item (e.g., its net cost and status). After you have implemented the inventory database, you will write queries to generate some of the reports the JKC users need to perform their jobs more effectively.

■ **Step I: Problem Analysis**   The first step is to analyze the **user requirements** to make sure that you understand the required functions of the PIMS database. The following questions ask you to analyze these requirements from various perspectives.

1. Define what you think will be the most important uses of the PIMS database for each of the users listed below. The designers' use(s) are provided as an example.
    a. *The Designers:* In a nutshell, the designers' most important concern is that the system provide an accurate and up-to-date picture of JKC's plant availability. The designers will use reports generated from the inventory database to determine whether plants are readily available to be used in their designs.

    b. Chip Kehrwald

    c. Anne Rogers

    d. Bob Edwards

2. Define a set of user requirements that you believe will be acceptable to all of the people listed in Exercise 1. To do this, you will need to identify each person's perspective on the input, processing, output, and storage (IPOS) requirements of the PIMS database. The designers' perspective is sketched below as an example.

The Designers' PIMS Database Requirements:

- *Input:* When a designer completes a design bid, s/he will give a copy of the bid to Anne. Any time a designer alters a design to exclude plants, s/he will alert Anne to change the bid status of those plants from "on bid" to "open."
- *Processing:* The designers' primary processing needs involve sorting plant records by plant type, expected delivery date, or other sort keys to generate reports about availability.
- *Output:* The designers need an up-to-date listing of items in JKC's inventory, including each item's current status: in-stock/open, in-stock/on-bid, on-order/open, or on-order/on-bid. For items on order, they need to know the expected delivery date.
- *Storage:* To satisfy the designers' needs, the following data must be stored about each plant item—plant description, plant size, plant ID number (a number assigned to each plant to distinguish it from other plants of its type), plant net cost, plant inventory status ('in-stock' or 'on-order'), order delivery date (if plant is on order), plant bid status ('on-bid' or 'open'), and bidder (if plant is on-bid).

3. Consolidate the individual user requirements to produce a list of all the IPOS requirements of the PIMS database.

■ **Step II: Database Design**   Assume that JKC has acquired the hardware to support the PIMS database. Assume also that JKC has purchased a relational DBMS that will allow them to store data as tables. The principles of good database design dictate that each table should contain data about only one **entity** or object (e.g., a generic person, place, thing, or event). For a review of data modeling terms and concepts, see Appendix DB1.

1. Anne, having studied some of the principles of relational DBMS design, can't decide how many **tables** are needed in the database. On the one hand, she thinks that only one table is needed; this table would list all the attributes of each plant in inventory. On the other hand, she thinks that two tables may be needed—one for plant types and one for plants—because JKC needs to maintain data both about plant categories (e.g., description, size, annual sales, supplier) and about specific plants (e.g., plant item number, net cost, inventory status). In this second approach, the two tables would be related to each other by plant code, a "made up" abbreviation for each plant type, e.g., "lacco" for laccospadix australasica palm. What are the advantages and disadvantages of each of these approaches?

2. Assume that Anne decided that the two-table design was better. Review the case description of the existing system and the storage requirements you identified in Step I. As you review this information, consider which data elements logically "belong to" a plant type and which "belong to" a specific plant in inventory or on order. Then answer the following questions.
   a. JKC's current manual system maintains data only about each plant type, not about specific plants. List the data (i.e., **attributes**) currently maintained about each plant type. Will all of this data need to be stored in the plant type table of the new system?

b. Identify any additional data about plant type that the users want maintained. Determine the **key identifier(s)** for the plant type table.

c. Identify the data that users need about each plant in inventory or on order. Determine the key identifier(s) of the plant item table.

d. Model these two tables using one of the data modeling techniques (e.g., entity-relationship diagram, conceptual data model, or any other modeling technique you've learned; see Appendix DB1 for more information about data modeling.). Show each entity's key identifier(s) and attributes, and indicate the **relationship** between the two tables.

3. Now that you have identified the data to be stored in the database, you need to describe the **physical file structure** of each table. List the field names for each file, and then identify each field's type (e.g., character, numeric, date) and width.

■ **Step III: Database Implementation and Report Generation**   You're now ready to begin implementing the PIMS database. Use your chosen DBMS to perform the exercises listed below.

1. Following the physical design you outlined in Step II, create and save the physical file structures. Then enter and save 20 plant-type records using the data provided in Tables 1 and 2, where appropriate. Finally, create 40 plant-item records; you will need to make up values for many of the fields in this file (e.g., item number, inventory status, bid status). Print a listing of the contents of each file.

2. Query your plant type file to print the following reports:
   a. A report listing the plant types for which Palms is the preferred supplier.

   b. A report listing the plant type, size, and average net cost for all plant types that have an average net cost over $200. Sort these report items in ascending order by net cost.

   c. A report listing the plant types available in 14-inch or 17-inch size, along with their average net costs and preferred suppliers.

3. Query your plant item file to print the following reports:
   a. A report listing the plant code, item number and inventory status of all plants on bid.

b. A report listing the plant code, item number, and net cost of all plants that are currently in-stock and not on-bid.

c. A report listing the plant code, item number, and expected delivery date of all plants currently on-order, sorted in ascending order by delivery date.

d. An Inventory Tax Report listing the plant code, item number, and individual net cost of all plants in-stock grouped on plant type with a subtotal for each type and the total net cost of all plants in-stock.

4. The reports in this exercise require you to link your plant type and plant item files to print the following reports:
    a. A report listing the plant type, size, and item number for all plants currently in-stock sorted by plant code.

    b. A report listing the plant code, item number, and preferred supplier for all plants currently on-order sorted by delivery date.

    c. A report listing the plant description, size, item number, and net cost for all plants currently not on-bid sorted by plant code.

5. Verify that the reports generated in Exercises 2, 3, and 4 above are correct by manually determining the expected output from your file listings and comparing the expected output to the generated output.

■ **Step IV: Post-Implementation Review**   Having developed your inventory database system, you now need to evaluate how well it satisfies user requirements and what kinds of enhancements should be recommended to better improve business efficiency and effectiveness.

1. Review the **user requirements** you identified in Step I. Discuss how well your system fulfills these requirements.

2. Businesses implement information systems to improve their efficiency and effectiveness. Consider each of the users identified in Step I. Does your system make these users more productive or improve the quality of their work? Does your system contribute to JKC's effectiveness—for example, by improving its ability to compete? Does the system help JKC achieve its **critical success factors**? Critical success factors are the things that a business must do right in order to ensure its survival.

3. Assume that JKC's Plant Inventory Management System (PIMS) cost $25,000 to implement, including hardware and software costs, Eric's consulting fees, and Anne's labor. Do the improvements in effectiveness and efficiency (i.e., the benefits of the PIMS) justify this investment?

4. Michael Hammer, a researcher and consultant specializing in **business process reengineering,** has noted that too many information systems development projects just focus on "paving the cowpaths" instead of innovating better business processes with information technology. The focus in business process reengineering is to redesign business processes for greater efficiency and effectiveness. Does your system just "pave the cowpaths," or does it support innovative business practices? Explain your answer.

5. Chip and Elizabeth have opted to evolve an integrated information system over time. Recommend system enhancements and/or modifications to improve the extent to which PIMS contributes to JKC's efficiency and effectiveness. Recommend both short-range (i.e., in the next 6–12 months) and long-range (i.e., in the next 1–3 years) modifications.

6. Write a short memo (about 2 pages) to Chip and Elizabeth in which you address Questions 1–5.

Case 6:
An Inventory Management System for JKC

Part B:

Inventory Management Decision Model

Learning Objectives

The purpose of this case is to demonstrate how a business can improve its **efficiency** and **effectiveness** by implementing a decision model to manage its procurement costs. Specifically, in this case you will:

1. Define the problem to be solved by specifying **user requirements.**
2. Use a spreadsheet tool to develop a **decision model** that determines the **economic order quantity** and **economic reorder point** for inventory.
3. Examine the business benefits of this inventory management system.

■ **Spreadsheet Skills Required**

Basic

1. Format a worksheet by entering headings and labels and specifying column width and cell type/format.
2. Write formulas to sum a range of cells.
3. Copy formulas using **absolute and relative cell references.**

Advanced

4. Use **square root** and **table lookup** functions.
5. Perform What if…? analyses by modifying decision model assumptions.

We assume that students already possess all the spreadsheet skills listed above except #4, which is discussed in the case exercises.

Background

As noted in Part A of this case, Jenson-Kehrwald Company (JKC) is a partnership, owned by Elizabeth Jenson and Chip Kehrwald. JKC designs and develops interior landscapes for hotels, restaurants, condominiums, and large private estates.

One of the critical success factors for JKC is inventory management. They must have appropriate plants available when needed; however, because their inventory is expensive to maintain, they do not want more inventory than necessary. But with order lead time averaging 4 weeks, they need to maintain sufficient stock to carry them until the ordered items are delivered.

Elizabeth and Chip hired a business consultant, Eric Diehl, to suggest ways to improve JKC's inventory management processes. As Eric analyzed these processes, he found that JKC was incurring unreasonably high procurement and inventory costs because it had no formal process for determining the optimal order and inventory quantities for each item.

■ Table 1

Suppliers, Lead Times, and Sales for Each Plant Type

DESC	Size	Sales/Yr	AveNet$	Supplier1	Supplier2
laccospadix australasica palm	15 gal	50	$450.00	Palms(4)	Lunds(5)
arenga pinnata palm	15 gal	80	$310.00	GPC(2)	Greens(3)
chamaedorea falcifera palm	15 gal	35	$300.00	Palms(4)	Lunds(5)
ceratozamia molongo palm	14"	85	$240.00	Palms(4)	Lunds(5)
arecastum coco plumosa	15 gal	135	$275.00	Greens(3)	GPC(2)
caryota mitis	7 gal	170	$140.00	Olsen(3)	Greens(3)
phoenix robellini	14"	155	$105.00	Lunds(5)	Greens(3)
chamaedorea "bamboo"	14"	115	$110.00	China(8)	Palms(9)
raphis palm	14"	135	$350.00	Palms(4)	Lunds(5)
spath deneve	14"	175	$ 90.00	Greens(3)	GPC(2)
corynocarpus leav	16"	200	$130.00	Greens(3)	GPC(2)
ti character	10 gal	120	$155.00	TisRUs(7)	Olsen(9)
red ti character	7 gal	135	$140.00	TisRUs(7)	Olsen(9)
green ti	7 gal	180	$140.00	TisRUs(7)	Olsen(9)
j c compacta	3 gal	250	$ 55.00	GPC(2)	Lunds(5)
green ti	5 gal	160	$ 92.00	TisRUs(7)	Olsen(9)
raphis palm	3 gal	150	$180.00	Palms(4)	Lunds(5)
ficus green gem	14"	200	$ 90.00	Figs(4)	Lunds(5)
ficus green gem	17"	100	$240.00	Figs(4)	Lunds(5)
marginata	2 gal	230	$ 45.00	GPC(2)	Greens(3)

Chip is responsible for maintaining inventory. Currently, he uses the "gut feeling" approach—based on an overview of historical sales and a forecast of future needs—to determine how many of each plant to order and when to place an order.

As shown in Table 1, Chip maintains data about each plant type's preferred and back-up suppliers with their order lead times (shown in parentheses beside supplier name), and annual sales. But he relies largely on "instinct" when deciding the quantity and timing for each order.

Eric has recommended that JKC implement a worksheet decision model to help them reduce their ordering and inventory costs. A **decision model** is a mathematical representation of a situation, which is used to facilitate decision making about that situation. For example, decision models are used in business to schedule production runs, to set product prices, and to determine the best location for a new plant.

In this exercise, you will construct a decision model to determine the economic order quantity and economic reorder point for each plant type. The **economic order quantity (EOQ)** is the quantity of a stock item that a firm should order at one time to minimize its costs of both **procurement** (the process of ordering and receiving goods) and storage and to reduce the amount of capital it has tied up in inventory.

The formula for calculating the EOQ is

$$\text{SQRT}((2 * \text{procurement cost})/\text{inventory cost rate}) *$$
$$\text{SQRT}(\text{annual unit sales}/\text{unit cost})$$

where SQRT indicates the square root. The **economic reorder point (ERP)** indicates the stock level at which an item should be reordered to avoid stock-outs.

The formula for calculating the ERP is

$$\text{order lead time} * \text{weekly unit sales}$$

where **order lead time** is the number of weeks from the date of placing an order to the date of receiving it and weekly unit sales is the annual unit sales divided by 52. By determining the EOQ and ERP for each plant type, JKC can more effectively manage its inventory and reduce the costs of purchasing and storing its stock.

Working with Chip, Eric studied JKC's procurement and inventory carrying processes and identified the costs shown in Table 2. These costs must be known in order to determine the appropriate order and inventory quantities for each plant type. Also needed are the average net cost and annual sales for each plant type, as shown in Table 1.

■ Table 2	**Procurement Costs**		**Inventory Cost Rate***	
Procurement and Inventory	Communications	$25.00	Storage / Maintenance	12%
Costs for JKC	Labor	$40.00	Taxes / Insurance	3%
	Supplies	$7.50	Depreciation	2%
	Miscellaneous	$5.00	Interest	9%
	Total	$77.50	Total	26%

*Inventory Cost Rate is represented as a percentage of the plant type's net cost.
For example, if a plant type's net cost is $100, its inventory cost is $26.

■ QUESTIONS AND EXERCISES

■ **Step I: Problem Analysis**   The first step is to analyze the **user requirements** to make sure that you understand the required functions of the PIMS decision model. The following questions ask you to analyze these requirements.

1. Who are the users of the decision model?

2. What business processes will the decision model support? Think here in terms of **operational and management control** and **strategic planning.** Which of these is the decision model supposed to support? How?

3. Analyze the user requirements of the decision model system by identifying its inputs, processing, and outputs.

■ **Step II: Worksheet Design** You will begin design of this worksheet by first determining what data is needed to calculate the economic order quantity and the economic reorder point. Then you will design the layout of your worksheet; format it with column headings; enter the required data or import data from the plant type table constructed in Part A; and then enter the formulas, tables, and other components needed to perform the calculations.

You should assume that Chip wants a single worksheet that lets him calculate and display the EOQ and ERP for all of the plant types. Thus, a major section of your worksheet will contain a row of values for each of the 20 plant types. See Appendix SS1 for tips on designing your worksheet.

1. List the general identifying information about each plant type that should be provided in your worksheet. Determine a column heading, column width, cell type, and cell format for each data element.

2. List the data elements needed to calculate and display the EOQ for each plant type. Determine a column heading, column width, cell type, and cell format for each data element.

3. List the data elements needed to calculate and display the ERP for each plant type. Determine a column heading, column width, cell type, and cell format for each data element.

4. On a sheet of graph paper, sketch the layout of your worksheet, indicating column headings, column widths, and cell types/formats for all the plant type and EOQ/ERP columns.

5. Table 2 shows that the procurement costs and inventory cost rate are the same for all plant types. However, these individual costs/ percentages are subject to change, for example, if labor wages or interest rates increase. Thus, you should include a breakdown of these costs in a separate section of your worksheet. Sketch the placement of this cost table in your worksheet layout design. Indicate a label, cell type, and cell format for each data element.

■ Step III: Worksheet Implementation

Building the Worksheet Skeleton / Entering Plant Type Data

If you completed the database exercises in this case (Part A), begin your implementation activities at #1 below; if not, begin at #2.

1. Having created the plant type table in Part A above will save you some time as you create your worksheet because you will be able to import your plant type data from your database into your worksheet. The following import procedure assumes that you are using Lotus 1-2-3; if you are using a different spreadsheet product, consult your user manual for instructions on how to import data into a spreadsheet.
   a. To begin, select the **TRANSLATE** function from the Lotus 1-2-3 Access menu.[1]

      At the prompt asking you what product you want to **TRANSLATE FROM,** select the appropriate source file type (e.g., dBase III).

---

[1] To access this menu, you should boot the program by entering the command **lotus** (not **123**) at the system prompt.

b. At the next prompt asking you what product you want to **TRANSLATE TO,** select the appropriate target file type (e.g., Lotus 1-2-3, version 2.3).

c. When asked to enter the name of the **SOURCE FILE** to be translated, enter the name of the file containing your plant type table. When asked to enter the name of the worksheet file you want this data saved to, enter a name for your worksheet.

d. Now get into your worksheet by selecting **123** from the Access menu. Load your worksheet (**/FR**).
   Your plant type data will be displayed with field names used as column headings and field values displayed under these headings. Each row will contain the data from one plant type record. The cell contents will be unformatted. Thus, you will need to do some "cleaning up" to make the data easy to read; but at least you won't have to retype all the data!

e. Review your worksheet layout design plan to determine whether any of these columns of data should be deleted. For example, your plant type table included the names and lead times for both preferred and backup suppliers. You need to use only the lead times of preferred suppliers in your worksheet.

f. Delete all unneeded columns, and then finish formatting your worksheet by entering additional column headings, setting column widths/formats, etc.

When you have finished constructing the skeleton of your worksheet and are ready to begin entering your procurement/inventory cost table and EOQ/ERP formulas, proceed to #3 below.

2. If you didn't complete the database exercises in Part A, you should begin constructing your worksheet by building its "skeleton."
   a. Refer to your worksheet layout design and enter column headings, set column widths and formats, etc.

   b. Enter the appropriate data for each of the 20 plant types described in the case tables. You should use the lead time indicated for the preferred suppliers in Table 1 as the lead time for each plant type.

When you have finished constructing the skeleton of your worksheet and are ready to begin entering your procurement/inventory cost table and EOQ/ERP formulas, proceed to #3 below.

Entering Procurement and Inventory Cost Tables

3. Leave a few blank rows beneath your plant data.
   a. Build the table for procurement costs, using appropriate labels and entering the procurement cost data provided in Table 2. Use a formula to calculate total procurement costs so that you can change individual costs if necessary.

b. Build the table for inventory cost rate, using appropriate labels and entering the inventory cost rate data provided in Table 2. Use a formula to calculate the total inventory cost rate so that you can change individual rates if necessary.

Entering Formulas for EOQ and ERP

At this point, your decision model should contain all the data needed to calculate the EOQ and ERP for each plant type: total procurement cost, total inventory cost rate, and the annual sales, unit cost, and lead time of each plant type. Verify that your worksheet contains values for all of these data elements.

To calculate the EOQ for each plant type, you will need to use the **@SQRT** function (square root) and to multiply and/or divide the contents of a number of cells. In the EOQ formula, the cells containing values that are constant for all plant types (e.g., total procurement cost) should be referenced as absolute cells. In most spreadsheets, an **absolute cell reference** includes a dollar sign before the column and row numbers, for example, A25; an absolute cell reference always refers to the same cell, even if the formula is copied to another location. Cells whose values vary depending on plant type (e.g., annual sales) should be entered in formulas as **relative cell references,** for example, simply as A25.

Because the EOQ formula is the most complex one used in this worksheet, we'll help you out by giving you an example. Recall that the formula for computing the EOQ is

$$SQRT((2 * procurement\ cost)/inventory\ cost\ rate)$$
$$* SQRT(annual\ unit\ sales/unit\ cost)$$

In our sample formula, we make the following assumptions:

1. The value for total procurement costs is located in cell B36.
2. The value for total inventory rate is located in cell B47.
3. The annual sales of laccospadix palms is located in cell D6.
4. The average unit cost of this plant type is located in cell E6.

Given these assumptions, the formula for calculating the EOQ is

$$@SQRT((2*\$B\$36)/\$B\$47)*@SQRT(D6/E6)$$

which yields an EOQ of 8 for laccospadix australasica palms.

5. Now use the example above to write the EOQ formula.
   a. Adjust the example formula for your spreadsheet product and your worksheet layout. Then enter it in the appropriate cell for laccospadix australasica palms.

   b. Verify that the correct value was generated. Now copy this formula to the rest of the cells in the EOQ column. If you copied the formula correctly, you should have the value 55 as the EOQ for marginata.

6. Now move your cursor to the cell for laccospadix australasica palm's ERP.
   a. Enter the formula for calculating the economic reorder point (ERP). Recall that the ERP formula is

   *order lead-time * weekly unit sales*

   where weekly unit sales is the annual unit sales divided by 52. Because this is a relatively simple formula, we'll let you do it on your own.

   b. To verify that your formula is correct and that it has been copied correctly, check to make sure that the ERP for laccospadix australasica palms is 4 and for marginata is 9.

7. Print your completed worksheet.

Performing What If . . . ? Analysis and Enhancing Your Worksheet

One of the advantages of using spreadsheets to maintain data and to perform calculations is that you can easily manipulate the data to investigate various scenarios. What if marginata is written up in a major interior design magazine and becomes the *tres chic* plant for interior landscaping? If you anticipate that sales this year will double over last year's total, how will this sales growth affect the EOQ and ERP? What if your workers go on strike for higher wages and the labor cost of procuring stock rises 30 percent? What if...?

Exercises 7–9 present three scenarios that JKC may encounter and asks you to manipulate your worksheet data to predict how each scenario would affect JKC's EOQ and ERP. Exercise 10 asks you to modify your worksheet to perform additional calculations. Before you complete these exercises, we recommend that you save a backup copy of your worksheet just in case your manipulations wreak havoc! What if you accidently delete a column...? What if you screw up a formula...? What if ...?

7. We must be clairvoyant! Just last week *Interior Design* ran a cover photo and lead story on the "Queen of Versatility"—marginata. Now JKC's phones are ringing off the hook as customers call to request that their *tres gauche* greens be ripped out and replaced with blankets of the Queen. Chip predicts that marginata will be a hot seller for the next year, tripling (OK, we underestimated the herd instinct of the American consumer) last year's sales of marginata.
   a. Adjust your data appropriately.

   b. What are the new values for marginata's EOQ and ERP?

8. Given the burgeoning popularity of marginata, Chip is having an increasingly difficult time locating suppliers for the plant. And when he does find a supplier, he also finds that the unit cost has doubled. Chip estimates that the communication and labor costs for procuring marginata are twice the usual costs.
   a. Adjust your data to reflect not only the tripling of sales (as in #7) but also the doubling of unit cost and communication and labor procurement costs.

   b. What are the new values for marginata's EOQ and ERP?

9. Tis-R-Us, JKC's preferred supplier for all ti plants, has gone out of business. Now JKC must get its ti stock from Olsen Suppliers, which has a lead time of 9 weeks.
   a. Adjust your worksheet data to reflect this change. (If you changed procurement costs, etc., in Exercises 7–8, be sure to return these data elements to their original values before executing the lead time change!)

   b. What are the new EOQ and ERP values for each ti plant type?

10. Chip has read that many businesses include safety stock in their ERP calculations and wants you to modify your decision model to include this factor. **Safety stock** is the desired minimum quantity of a unit on hand when an order arrives; in other words, it's a cushion against stockouts caused by unexpectedly high sales or long delivery times. Although safety stock helps a company avoid stockouts, it also raises the inventory carrying costs; thus, a business must strike a balance between its desire to avoid stockouts and its need to avoid incurring unnecessarily high carrying costs. Your task is to modify your worksheet to include safety stock in your ERP.

    a. First, make sure that your worksheet contains the original plant type and cost data values. Later on, we will give you some of the safety stock values so that you can verify your formulas. These verification values are derived from the *original* worksheet data, not from the changes you may have made to your worksheet in Exercises 7–9.

    b. Next, insert a column for Safety Stock in your worksheet, and add a heading for this column.

    c. To calculate the safety stock quantity, you must implement another table in your worksheet. This table includes two columns: desired stockout protection levels and their corresponding stockout multipliers. The **stockout protection level** indicates the degree of certainty that you will not experience a stockout. For example, a stockout protection level of 95% means that you can be 95% certain that you will not run out of that item before the next order arrives. The **stockout multiplier** is used to calculate the quantity of safety stock needed given a particular stockout protection level. These values are shown in Table 3. We recommend that you locate this table to the right of your procurement/inventory costs table. Go ahead and construct the table, using appropriate column headings and entering the values provided in Table 3.

■ Table 3	Stockout Protection Level	Stockout Multiplier
Stockout Multiplier Table	10%	−1.28
	20%	−0.84
	30%	−0.52
	40%	−0.25
	50%	0
	60%	0.25
	70%	0.52
	80%	0.84
	90%	1.28
	95%	1.65
	98%	2.05
	99%	3.08

d. Above or below your stockout multiplier table, create a label "Safety Level:" as a prompt so that the user can indicate the stockout protection level desired. In the cell immediately to the right of this label, the user will enter the stockout protection level desired.

e. To select the multiplier corresponding to the stockout protection level indicated by the user, you need to treat your stockout multiplier table as a **lookup table.** A lookup table pairs a given value for one data element with a corresponding value for another data element. Creating the table is easy, as you saw in completing (c) above. But writing the formula to access a particular stockout multiplier is more difficult. Because this is a somewhat complicated task that you may have never performed before, we'll help you out by providing an example. The assumptions in our example are listed below:

1. The stockout protection level value was entered in cell D52.

2. The stockout multiplier table is located in cells C55..D66.

3. The stockout multiplier is one vertical column to the right of the stockout protection level.

Given these assumptions, the function for looking up the stockout multiplier is

@VLOOKUP(D52,C55..D66,1)

where D52 is the address of the cell containing the value to be matched, C55..D66 indicates the range in which the lookup table is located, and 1 indicates that the stockout multiplier value to be returned is one vertical column to the right of the column of stockout protection level values.

Review your lookup table placement, and adjust our sample formula to reflect your table placement. To verify that your formula works, enter a stockout protection level of 80% at the "Safety Level:" prompt. Then move your cursor to the laccospadix australasica palms Safety Stock cell on your worksheet, and enter the VLOOKUP formula. The value that appears in the cell should be .84.

f. Now that you've verified your VLOOKUP formula, you need to modify it to calculate the safety stock quantity. The formula for calculating this is

stockout multiplier * SQRT(lead time * weekly sales)

where your @VLOOKUP formula should be substituted for the stockout multiplier. If you've written the formula correctly, the safety stock quantity for laccospadix australasica palms will be 2.

g. Copy your safety stock formula to the cells for the other plant types. If you copied your formula correctly, the safety stock quantity for marginata will be 2.

h. As currently implemented, your economic reorder point formula assumes a safety stock quantity of zero. Adjust your ERP formula to include the safety stock quantity. If you've made the correct adjustment, the new ERP for laccospadix australasica palms will be 5.

i. Print your modified worksheet.

j. Reset the stockout protection level to 95%. What are the new safety stock and ERP values for laccospadix australasica palms? At what stockout protection level does the safety stock for all plant types equal zero?

■ **Step IV: Post-Implementation Review**   Now that you've implemented and manipulated your PIMS decision model worksheet, you should have some insights into how this decision model will help Chip manage JKC's inventory more efficiently and more effectively.

1. Review the user requirements you identified in Step I. How well does your worksheet satisfy these requirements and support JKC's business processes?

2. Businesses implement information systems to improve their **efficiency** and **effectiveness.** Consider each of the users identified in Step I. Does your system make these users more productive or improve the quality of their work? Does your system contribute to JKC's effectiveness, e.g., by improving its ability to achieve its **critical success factors?**

3. Assume that JKC's Plant Inventory Management System (PIMS) cost $25,000 to implement, including hardware and software costs, Eric's consulting fees, and Anne's labor. Do the improvements in effectiveness and efficiency (i.e., the benefits of the PIMS) justify this investment?

4. Write a short memo (about 2 pages) to Chip and Elizabeth in which you address Questions 1–3.

5. Review your answers to Implementation Exercises 7–9. Demonstrate your understanding of the calculations performed by answering the following questions:
   a. In Exercise 7, both EOQ and ERP were affected when you changed the annual unit sales of marginata. Why?

   b. In Exercise 8, only the EOQ was affected by your manipulations. Why?

   c. In Exercise 9, only the ERP was affected by your manipulations. Why?

Spreadsheet Appendices

The spreadsheet appendices describe some of the more advanced Lotus 1-2-3 procedures required to complete the exercises. Because many spreadsheets perform the same operations (e.g., formatting cells, copying a range of cells), use the same keywords (e.g., SUM to sum a range of cells), and enforce the same syntax (e.g., A12 to indicate an absolute cell reference), many of the basic concepts presented here translate to different spreadsheet products. The primary difference will be in the structure of the user interface (e.g., Microsoft Excel's pull-down menus vs. Lotus's menu bars). To be safe, *consult your user manual* if you are using a spreadsheet other than Lotus 1-2-3.

Several notational conventions used in the spreadsheet appendices are described below:

/	The slash key is used to activate the Lotus menu.
FS OTF	Letters shown in all upper-case and bold-face type are Lotus commands; they should be typed when you want to access a command from Lotus's command menus. As you type these commands, you may use either upper- or lower-case letters. You DO NOT need to press [Enter] after typing these letters.
savefile	Words shown in bold-faced lower-case or mixed-case letters are to be typed as part of a command procedure.
<u>documentation</u>	Underlined words shown in bold-faced lower-case or mixed-case letters are terms that are defined in the text.
[ESC]	Special keys are shown in square brackets.
<filename>	Lower-case words enclosed in angle brackets indicate that you are to substitute the name of a file.
Create	Words in italics indicate menu selections or options.

Whenever a process description calls for you to "enter" a formula or label, you need to type the formula or label and then press the [Enter] key. Whenever a process description calls for you to "select" an option from a menu, you can (1) type the first letter of the command, or (2) use your cursor movement keys to highlight the desired menu option and then press the [Enter] key.

Appendix SS1:
Tips on Constructing and Printing
A Worksheet

Throughout the exercises, we offer suggestions on how to lay out your worksheets. In this appendix, we present a more unified discussion of worksheet design. One of the overriding guidelines in worksheet design is "Whenever possible, design your worksheet to look like its paper document equivalent." For example, if you are constructing a financial statement worksheet, try to make your worksheet look as much like the typical financial statement as possible. Doing so will facilitate user understanding of your worksheet.

Sections of a Worksheet

When there is no standard paper equivalent of the worksheet you are constructing, we suggest you organize your worksheet in four sections: identification, input/assumptions, calculations/output, and documentation. The **identification section,** which should be included in every worksheet, lists the file name, author, creation or last modification date, and a brief description of the worksheet. Typically, this section should appear at the upper lefthand corner of your worksheet. Each identifying piece of information should appear on a separate line. A few blank rows should separate the identification section from the next section.

The **input/assumptions section** appears below the identification section and provides the raw data used in your spreadsheet; for example, in the Jefferson Dance Club case, the tables of lessons per hour are raw data that should appear in your input/assumptions section. Also appearing in this section are any variable assumptions that the user can control. For example, in the Starlight Expeditions case, you need to manipulate food costs and attendance. You may want to provide a "Food Cost Factor" label cell and a cell in which the user can enter the assumed value—for example, 80 percent. Providing for variable assumptions will facilitate What if . . . ? analyses.

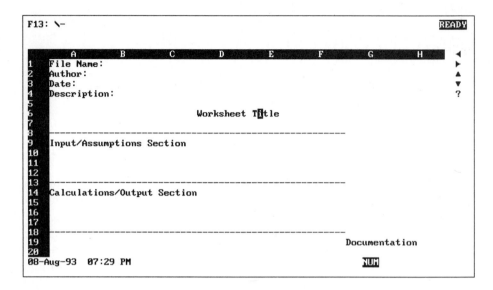

The **calculations/output section** is located below or to the right of the input/assumptions section. In this section, you include labels and formulas to calculate and display the desired outputs. The last section, **documentation**, is generally located in a worksheet area that will not be affected if you insert or delete columns or rows. Thus, this section usually appears to the right and below the other sections of your worksheet. The documentation section provides definitions of key terms, instructions for using the worksheet, and/or macros to make using the worksheet easier.

Using Titles, Labels, and Column Headings

To improve the readability of your worksheet, be sure to provide ample titles, labels, and column headings. You should title your worksheet, just as you would title a report, centering the title above the worksheet and, where appropriate, underlining it for emphasis. The title is provided *in addition to* the worksheet information of the identification section and should be descriptive; for example, "Financial Model of Jefferson Dance Club" is much more descriptive than "Worksheet 1." In addition, every input cell should have a descriptive label, and every column of inputs or outputs should have a column heading to describe the nature of the data contained in the column.

Avoid using abbreviations in titles, labels, and headings, if possible. The exception to this rule is that you should feel free to use standard abbreviations if there's little doubt that your users will understand them. For example, the meaning of the abbreviation "GR" is obscure; as the person who constructed the worksheet, you may know that it represents "Gross Revenue," but no one else will. In contrast, if the worksheet is designed for business users, most will recognize "ROI" as "Return on Investment" and "GNP" as "Gross National Product," and almost any user will interpret "#" as "Number."

Formatting Labels and Setting Column Widths

Use the formatting features of Lotus liberally to improve the readability of your worksheet. The *Range Format* **(/RF)** submenu lists a number of formatting options, including percentage and currency, which can greatly improve the appearance of your worksheet. Another formatting guideline is to avoid crowding too much data into too small an area. You can easily change the alignment of column headings and labels to improve your worksheet's appearance. To change label alignment, move the cell pointer to the beginning cell of the range you want to reformat, and select *Range Label Right* **(/RLR)** and highlight the cells to be reformatted to right-justify your labels. You can also center **(/RLC)** or left-justify **(/RLL)** your labels.

   Use the *Worksheet Column Set Width* **(/WCS)** command to set column widths that leave at least a few blank spaces between column entries. Use blank rows or provide underlining or a row of stars (*) to separate sections of the worksheet. You can quickly fill a cell with hyphens (-) or stars by moving the cell pointer to the cell and typing \- or *. If your worksheet includes several models (e.g., as in Jefferson Dance Club, where you repeat your financial analysis for several scenarios), you can improve readability by "boxing" each model. Use \- to create the horizontal box lines; to create the vertical box lines, enter | (located on the backslash key of most keyboards) in the first column cell, and use the Copy function (/C) to fill the remaining vertical cells.

Using Absolute and Relative Cell References

Formulas used in a worksheet often contain a combination of absolute cell references and relative cell references. In Lotus 1-2-3, an **absolute cell reference** includes a dollar sign before the column and row numbers, for example, A25; an absolute cell reference always refers to the same cell, even if the formula is copied to another location. You use absolute cell references in formulas to refer to cells that contain constant data.

   A **relative cell reference** is represented simply by the column letter and row number, for example, simply as A25. A relative cell reference is one that is interpreted as a location relative to the current cell. For example, assume the formula @sum(A20.A24) is located in cell A25. Lotus interprets this formula as "sum the contents of the five cells directly above the current cell and place the result in the current cell." Thus, when you copy this formula to cell B25, the formula stored in B25 is @sum(B20.B24). You use relative cell references in formulas to refer to cells that contain variable data.

Printing a Worksheet in Sections

To print your worksheet in sections, you will need to identify the range of cells to be printed for each page. Review your worksheet to determine logical page breaks, and then perform the following procedure.

1. Type **/PP** to select the *Print* function from the Lotus menu and to direct the output to the printer.

2. Select *Range* **(R)** from the Print Settings menu. The cursor will move to the "Range:" prompt of the Print Settings screen.

3. Specify the range for the first page to be printed. You can specify a range of cells in one of two ways:
   (1) enter the cell range, for example, A1.H45 or
   (2) press [F6] to display the worksheet, and then use the cursor movement keys to highlight the portion of the worksheet you want to print; press [Enter].

4. Continue the printing procedure, aligning the top of the page, and so on as necessary. Select *GO* **(G)** to print your worksheet.

5. Repeat this process for each of the sections of your worksheet.

If each of your worksheet sections doesn't fit on one page, you may need to use **compressed type,** which prints a 132-character line. A common setup string used to tell many printers to use compressed type is 015. If your printer requires a different setup string, replace \015 with \<your printer setup string> in step #2 below. To print your worksheet using compressed type:

1. Select *Options Setup* **(OS)** from the Print menu.

2. Type **\015** and press [Enter].

3. Select *Margins Right* **(MR)** from the Options menu.

4. Type **132** and press [Enter].

5. Select *Quit* **(Q)** to leave the Options menu.

6. Continue the printing procedure, aligning the top of the page, and so on as necessary. Select *GO* **(G)** to print your worksheet. Repeat this process for each of the sections of your worksheet.

Appendix SS2:
Creating and Printing Graphs

Often times, no matter how effectively you design your worksheet, it will contain too much data for the user to comprehend easily. In these situations, you'll want to create graphs to encapsulate the most important information in your worksheet. In this appendix, we describe several graph types and their appropriate uses and then describe the procedures for creating and printing graphs.

Graph Types and Uses

The three basic types of graphs supported by Lotus 1-2-3 are line graphs, bar graphs, and pie charts. A **line graph** represents data as points in time, where the x-axis is a time line and the y-axis gives the quantity of the item being measured (e.g., dollar sales, units sold, number of students majoring in business). Thus, each point represents the value of the item being measured at a particular point in time. The points are connected to show the trend over time

■ **Figure A-2**

Line Graph

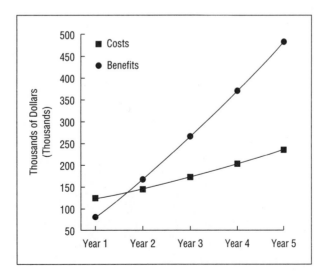

(e.g., increasing sales over the past year, fluctuations in sales by season, etc.). Multiple lines can be used to represent changes in multiple data values over time. When multiple lines are used, you need to include a **legend,** which associates each line style with the data it represents. Line graphs are very effective for illustrating trends in data over time.

A **bar graph** consists of a series of vertical or horizontal bars. In a simple bar graph, each bar represents one data component; for example, each bar represents the number of widgets sold in a particular month. Bars can be grouped to represent different components of a single situation (e.g., a group of three bars representing the number of widgets, whatsits, and gizmos sold in July; another group showing sales in August. Or they can be segmented to represent the percentage each component contributes to the total. For example, each bar on the graph represents the total sales of widgets, whatsits, and gizmos in a particular month; but each bar is divided into three sections to show the contribution of each product to total sales for that month. Bar graphs are especially effective for comparing figures for various time frames (e.g., sales by each computer manufacturer for several quarters or years) or for various scenarios (e.g., expected profits before and after a merger).

A **pie chart** consists of a "pie" sliced into various pieces. The size of the piece represents the percentage that each data component contributes to the whole (e.g., the percentage of sales that each department contributed to total store sales in the fourth quarter, or the percentage of each ethnic group in the U.S. population in 1990). Pie charts are especially useful any time you want to show percentages, that is, how components contribute to the whole.

■ **Figure A-3**

Bar Graph

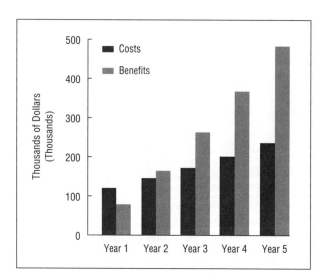

■ **Figure A-4**

Pie Chart

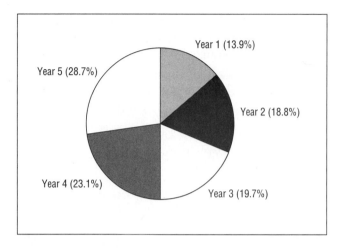

Creating a Graph

Your worksheet should have already been created and tested for completeness and accuracy before you begin the graph creation process.

1. Retrieve your worksheet file **(/FR).**

2. Select the graph function from the Lotus menu **(/G).** Most of the commands described below (except where otherwise indicated) are entered from the Graph menu.

3. Select *Reset Graph* **(RG)** to erase any previous graph settings.

Line and Bar Graphs

1. Select *Type* **(T)** from the Graph menu, and choose the type of graph you want to print (**B** for bar graph, **L** for line graph).

2. Select the X range **(X).** The X range indicates the labels to be placed on the X axis of your graph. Specify the X range by entering a cell range (e.g., A1.A10) or by highlighting the appropriate cell range on your worksheet and then pressing [Enter].

3. Type **A** to specify the A range: the range of cells containing a series of data to be graphed. Specify the A range by entering a cell range (e.g., A1.A10) or by highlighting the appropriate cell range on your worksheet and then pressing [Enter].

   If you want to display multiple series of data, for example, to build a multiple line graph, specify the B, C,..., F ranges. When you have finished specifying the data series, type **Q** to quit and return to the Graph menu.

4. To specify a title for your graph, select *Options Titles First* **(OTF)** from the Graph menu. Enter the first line of the title. If the title contains a second line, select *Titles Second* **(TS),** and enter the second title line.

5. To add a title for your y-axis, choose *Options Titles Yaxis* **(OTY)** from the Graph menu. Enter your title, and then press **Q** to return to the Graph menu.

6. To add a legend pairing a line or bar style to a particular data series, select *Options Legend A* **(OLA)** from the Graph menu. Then enter a legend label for data series A. Select *Legend B* **(LB)** to enter a legend label for data series B. Repeat this process for legends C–F as needed. Type **Q** to return to the Graph menu.

Pie Charts

1. Select *Type Pie* **(TP)** at the Graph menu.

2. The A range is used to specify the values to be assigned to the slices of your pie chart. Select *A* **(A)**, and specify the A range by entering a cell range (e.g., A1.A10) or by highlighting the appropriate cell range on your worksheet and then pressing [Enter].

3. The X range is used to specify labels for the slices of your pie chart. Select *X* **(X),** and specify the X range by entering a cell range (e.g.,

■ **Figure A-5**

Graph Menu

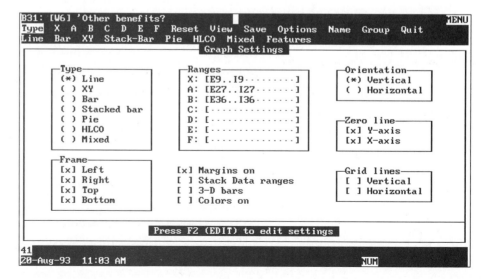

A1.A10) or by highlighting the appropriate cell range on your worksheet and then pressing [Enter].

4. Add a title for your pie chart by selecting *Options Title First* **(OTF)** at the Graph menu. Enter the first line of the title. If the title contains a second line, select *Titles Second* **(TS),** and enter the second title line. Select *Quit* **(Q)** to return to the Graph menu.

Viewing and Saving Graphs

1. To view your graph, select *View* **(V)** from the Graph menu. After viewing your graph, press any key to return to the Graph menu.

2. To name your graph, select *Name Create* **(NC)** from the Graph menu. The Graph Settings screen will appear. Enter the name of your graph. Naming your graph will save the graph settings as part of your worksheet.

3. To retrieve a named graph, first be sure that its corresponding worksheet has been retrieved and is displayed on the screen. Then select *Graph Name Use* **(/GNU)** from the Lotus menu. Lotus will display a list of named graphs associated with the active spreadsheet. Use the cursor movement keys to highlight the graph to be viewed, and press [Enter].

4. To save a graph for printing, first retrieve the graph to be saved by following the procedure outlined in #3. From the Graph menu, select *Save* **(S)** and enter a name for the graph.

■ **Figure A-6**

Lotus 1-2-3 Access Menu

```
 Create worksheets, graphs, and databases
 1-2-3       PrintGraph      Translate      Install      Exit


                              Lotus
                         1-2-3 Access Menu
                           Release 2.3

             Copyright 1990, 1991  Lotus Development Corporation
                        All Rights Reserved.

 To select a program to start, do one of the following:

     *  Use ←, →, HOME, or END to move the menu pointer
        to the program you want and then press ENTER.

     *  Type the first character of the program's name.

 Press F1 (HELP) for more information.
                                                          NUM
```

Printing Graphs

To print a graph, you need to start from the Lotus 1-2-3 **Access menu**. This menu is displayed when you boot the Lotus program by typing **lotus**—not **123** — at the system prompt. If you're already in Lotus, you will have to quit **(/QY)** and then enter **lotus** at the system prompt.

1. At the Access menu, select *PrintGraph* **(P)** to display the **PrintGraph menu** and current settings.
2. Select *Settings Hardware Graphs-Directory* **(SHG)** to indicate the disk drive where your graph files are saved. Enter **a:** or **b:** as appropriate. This is probably the only Hardware setting you need to change. Select *Quit* **(Q)** to return to the PrintGraph menu.
3. Select *Image-Select* **(I)** from the PrintGraph menu. The Select Graph to Print screen, giving a list of the graphs that have been saved for printing, will be displayed. Use the cursor movement keys to highlight the graph you want to print, and then press the space bar to mark your selection. A # sign will appear in front of the selected graph file.
4. Press [F10] to preview your graph. If you're satisfied with the way it looks, press any key to return to the Select Graph to Print screen. Then press [Enter] to finalize your selection. The name of your graph file will appear under the heading "Graphs to Print."
5. Select *Align Go* **(AG)** to print your graph. Then select *Page* **(P)** to advance the printer to the top of the next page.
6. When you've finished printing graphs, select *Exit Yes* **(EY)** to leave PrintGraph and return to the Access menu.

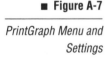

■ **Figure A-7**

PrintGraph Menu and Settings

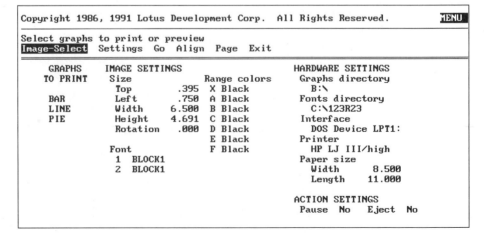

Appendix SS3:
Creating Macros

Some spreadsheet commands, such as saving or printing a worksheet and formatting a range of cells, are performed repeatedly as you construct and manipulate your worksheet. To save keystrokes, you can create a macro to automate some of these functions. A **macro** is a series of keystrokes and commands stored in a worksheet cell, much as you store a formula in a cell. In this appendix, we explain how to create and use your own macros.

Preliminaries

Representing Special Keys

Because macros often contain keystrokes that perform an action whenever they are typed—for example, pressing [Enter]—Lotus provides special conventions for representing these keystrokes. Most of the cursor-movement keys, functions keys, and special keys (e.g., "Delete," "Esc") are represented by the name or function of the key enclosed in curly brackets. For example, function key [F2] is represented as {edit}, the function it performs in Lotus. Similarly, function key [F5] is represented as {goto}, and [F6] as {window}; the upward cursor key as {up}, the left cursor key as {left}, the pageup key as {pageup}, and so on. The only keystroke not represented by its name or function is [Enter]; to represent this keystroke in a macro, you use the tilde (~) with no brackets.

Locating and Entering Your Macros

Macros should be placed in an area of your worksheet that is unlikely to be affected by inserted/deleted rows and columns. Thus, it is usually best to place your macros in cells located to the right and below your worksheet.

Each macro will consume at least three horizontal cells: one for its name, one for the macro itself, and one for a brief explanation of the macro's function. Macros are entered as labels; thus, each macro entry must begin with an apostrophe ('). The end of a macro instruction is indicated by a blank cell below the macro instruction. Thus, if you are creating several macros, you need to leave a blank cell between them.

Creating a Macro

Let's walk through an example to illustrate the process of creating a macro. Assume that we want to create two macros: one to save a worksheet and one to print a worksheet. Assume also that we will store the macros and their documentation in the range of cells R30…T35 and that we will name the first macro SAVEFILE and the second, PRINTFILE.

1. Locate the cell pointer in cell R30. Enter the name of the macro, **savefile.**

2. Move the cell pointer to cell S30. Type **'/fs~r** to represent the keystrokes required to save a file. Press [Enter].

3. Move the cell pointer to cell T30. Enter a brief statement of this macro's purpose, for example, **saves the file.**

4. Leave cell S31 blank to indicate the end of the SAVEFILE macro.

We will enter and store the more complex PRINTFILE macro in three pieces.

5. Locate the cell pointer in cell R32. Enter the second macro's name, **printfile.**

6. Move the cell pointer to cell S32. Type **'/PP** and press [Enter]. This piece of the macro accesses the Lotus menu and issues the print worksheet to printer command.

7. Move the cell pointer to cell T32. Enter a brief statement of what this piece of the macro does.

8. Move the cell pointer to cell S33. Type **'ra1.p45~** and press [Enter]. This piece of the macro specifies the print range.

9. Move the cell pointer to cell T33. Enter a brief statement of what this piece of the macro does.

10. Move the cell pointer to cell S34. Type **'agpq** and press [Enter].

This piece of the macro aligns the paper, prints the worksheet, formfeeds a new page, and quits the Print menu.

11. Move the cell pointer to cell T34, and enter a brief statement of what this piece of the macro does.

12. Leave cell S35 blank to indicate the end of this macro.

Naming a Macro

Macros can be named in one of two ways. The first way uses a backslash (\) followed by a single letter, for example, \s. Notice that the first character is a *back*slash, not the regular slash (/) used to activate the Lotus menu.

The second way to name a macro is to assign it a range name of up to 15 characters. In either case, you assign a name to your macro by performing the following procedure:

1. Place the cell pointer in the cell containing the macro.

2. Select *Range Name Create* **(/RNC)** from the Lotus menu.

3. Enter the name for your macro.

4. Press [Enter] again to indicate that you want to assign this name to the selected cell.

Thus, to name the SAVEFILE macro created above, you would

1. Place the cell pointer in S30.

2. Select *Range Name Create* **(/RNC)** from the Lotus menu.

3. Type **savefile** and press [Enter].

4. Press [Enter] again to indicate that you want to assign this name to the selected cell.

To name the PRINTFILE macro created above, you would

1. Place the cell pointer in S32, the beginning cell of this multi-cell macro.

2. Select *Range Name Create* **(/RNC)** from the Lotus menu.

3. Type **printfile** and press [Enter].

4. Press [Enter] again to indicate that you want to assign this name to the selected cell.

Running a Macro

The procedure you use to run a macro depends on the way you named it.

Macros Named with \

Press the [Alt] key and the letter key simultaneously.

Macros Named with a Range Name

1. Press the [Alt] key and the [F3] key simultaneously. A list of macro names will appear on the control panel.

2. Select the name of the macro from the list by highlighting it and pressing [Enter].

If you need to interrupt a macro while it is executing, press [Ctrl] [Break]. If this action causes the ERROR mode indicator (located in the upper righthand corner of your screen) to flash, press [Esc] to clear the error.

Database Appendices

The database appendices describe some of the more advanced procedures required to complete the exercises. Some of these procedures are described in the menu-based **Assistant mode;** others, in **dot prompt mode.** All procedures described in Assistant mode assume that you are using dBASE III+. All procedures described in dot prompt mode will work in dBASE III+ or in dBASE IV. In dBASE III+, you switch from the menu-based Assistant mode to the command-based dot prompt mode by pressing [Esc]; to return to Assistant mode, enter **ASSIST** at the dot prompt, or press [F2]. In dBASE IV, you switch from the menu-based Control Center mode to dot prompt mode by pressing [Esc] and entering **y** at the mode switch prompt; to return to Control Center, enter **ASSIST** at the dot prompt or press [F2].

Several notational conventions used in the database appendices are described below:

SELECT	Words shown in all upper-case letters and bold-faced type are reserved words in dBASE's command language; they should be typed where indicated in dot prompt mode. As you type these commands, you may use either upper- or lower-case letters.
y	Words shown in all lower-case letters and bold-faced type are text that you need to enter, e.g., at a prompt.
attribute	Words shown in underlined, bold-faced lower-case or mixed-case letters are terms that are defined in the text.
[ESC]	Special keys are shown in square brackets.
<source file>	Lower-case words enclosed in angle brackets indicate that you are to substitute the name of a field or file.
Create	Words in italics indicate menu selections or options. These are chosen from the dBASE menu when you are working in Assistant mode.

Whenever a process description calls for you to "enter" a command, you need to type the command and then press the [Enter] key; these process descriptions assume that you are working in dot prompt mode. Whenever a process description calls for you to "select" an option from a menu, you need to use your cursor movement keys to highlight the desired menu option and then press the [Enter] key; these process descriptions assume that you are working in Assistant mode.

Appendix DB1:
Data Modeling

Data **modeling** is a systems development activity in which you analyze an existing database or design a new one. Analyzing an existing database requires you to examine the source documents, reports, and any existing files of the application of interest. For example, if you were analyzing a sales order processing application, you would need to examine, at minimum, source documents such as the purchase order and invoice; any reports generated from this activity, such as sales by region or invoices outstanding; and the customer, product, and inventory records maintained to process sales. You would also need to consult with users and managers to learn what additional data they need and any special reports they would like to have.

Data modeling is usually performed in two steps. First, you define the things about which you need to maintain data and indicate how these things are related to each other. Modeling techniques for performing this step include the entity-relationship diagram (ERD) and the conceptual data model (CDM); we explain a variant of the conceptual data model here. Second, you use your ERD or CDM to define the tables of your database, each "thing" being represented as one table in your database. In some cases, it's feasible to skip the first step and go directly to the second. Nonetheless, we describe both steps here.

Conceptual Data Modeling

As you examine the source documents and reports and interview the users, you are trying to identify the entities in the users' application. An **entity** is a person, place, thing, or event about which data is collected and maintained. Examples of entities in a sales order processing system are CUSTOMER, PRODUCT, PURCHASE_ORDER, SALESPERSON, and INVOICE. Each of these entities is described by one or more **attributes:** the properties or characteristics that the user needs to know about each entity. For example, the entity CUSTOMER might be described by the attributes CustName, CustID,

CustStreet, CustCity, CustState, CustZip, and CustCreditLimit. In the CDM methodology, an entity and its corresponding attributes are represented using the following notation shown for PURCHASE_ORDER and CUSTOMER, respectively:

CUSTOMER

CustID	CustName	CustStreet	CustCity	CustState	CustZip	CustCLmt

PURCHASE_ORDER

PONumber	PODate	POAmt	POTerms

Notice that the name of an entity is given in all upper-case letters; the names of attributes are given in mixed-case letters. An **instance of an entity** consists of the values for the attributes that describe one entity; for example, H324T5, Dan Harding, 123 Elm Street, San Jose, CA, 95193, 5000.00 describes one instance of the CUSTOMER entity. An example of an instance of the PURCHASE_ORDER entity is PO17654, 02/11/95, 437.08, COD.

Each entity has at least one attribute that uniquely identifies it, that individuates it from all other instances of that entity. For example, the entity CUSTOMER is most likely uniquely identified by the attribute CustID. The attribute that uniquely identifies an entity is called the **key identifier** and is marked by underlining it as shown above. The value assigned to the attribute CustID—in this example, H324T5—is used to uniquely identify Dan Harding from Bill Jones or from another customer also named Dan Harding but whose CustID is H517F9. For PURCHASE_ORDER, the key identifiers are PONumber and PODate. Two attributes are needed here because different customers may submit purchase orders with the same numbers, but it's unlikely that different customers will submit purchase orders with the same PONumber and PODate.

Entities are related to each other in various ways. For example, in the sales order processing system, a CUSTOMER is related to a PURCHASE_ORDER in that a CUSTOMER submits a PURCHASE_ORDER. This **relationship** is indicated by a labeled line connecting the two entities, as shown below.

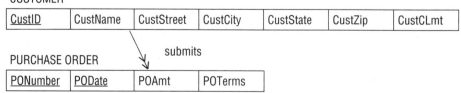

CUSTOMER

CustID	CustName	CustStreet	CustCity	CustState	CustZip	CustCLmt

submits

PURCHASE ORDER

PONumber	PODate	POAmt	POTerms

Relationships can be one-to-one, one-to-many, or many-to-many, and are represented using the following line types:

one-to-one	ENTITY A ———————————— ENTITY B
one-to-many	ENTITY A ———————————>> ENTITY B
many-to-many	ENTITY A <<———————————>> ENTITY B

Sometimes it is important to represent a relationship that may involve one instance of Entity A related to zero or more instances of Entity B. This relationship can be represented by drawing a circle on the end of the line connecting to the appropriate entity:

zero or one to one	ENTITY A ———————————— O –> ENTITY B
zero or one to many	ENTITY A ———————————— O –>> ENTITY B

The relationship between CUSTOMER and PURCHASE_ORDER is one to zero or many; each CUSTOMER submits zero to many PURCHASE_ORDERs. Reading the relationship in the opposite direction, each PURCHASE_ORDER is submitted by exactly one CUSTOMER. This relationship captures the real-world case in which customers may make purchases without submitting a purchase order (e.g., by coming into the store and paying cash); it also captures the business policy that each purchase order must be submitted by exactly one customer, a policy designed to facilitate billing and delivery.

In the conceptual data model, a **many-to-many relationship** requires special treatment. An example of a many-to-many relationship is that between PRODUCT and PURCHASE_ORDER: each product may be listed on many purchase orders, and each purchase order may list many products, as shown below.

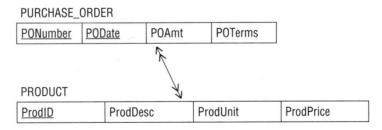

PURCHASE_ORDER

PONumber	PODate	POAmt	POTerms

PRODUCT

ProdID	ProdDesc	ProdUnit	ProdPrice

Many-to-many relationships require that we create a third entity—called an **intersection entity**—to represent the intersection of this relationship. In this case, the intersection entity is PO_LINE_ITEM, a line on the purchase order that lists all the data relevant to one product. Thus, the preferred way to represent the relationship between a PURCHASE_ORDER and a PRODUCT is

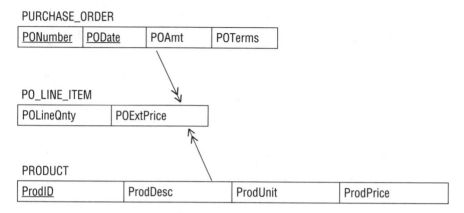

PURCHASE_ORDER

PONumber	PODate	POAmt	POTerms

PO_LINE_ITEM

POLineQnty	POExtPrice

PRODUCT

ProdID	ProdDesc	ProdUnit	ProdPrice

where the relationship between either of the other entities and the intersection entity is one-to-many. You may have noticed that none of the attributes of any of the entities is repeated in the conceptual data model; one rule of the CDM technique is that *each attribute may appear only once in the model.*

Building Database Tables

When we transform our conceptual data model into the tables of our database, the relationship lines between entities are omitted, and attributes are repeated to represent the relationships among the entities. In this transformation process, each entity in the conceptual data model is represented as a **table,** a matrix of columns (attributes or fields) and rows (entity instances or records). Now, *all* the pieces of data to be stored in each table are shown. To represent the relationship between CUSTOMER and PURCHASE_ORDER, we include the identifier of CUSTOMER—CustID—in the PURCHASE_ORDER table, as shown below with sample instances of each entity:

PURCHASE_ORDER

PONumber	PODate	POAmt	POTerms	CustID
ABC9087-95	02/01/95	2046.98	debit acct	A187B3
PO17654	02/11/95	437.08	COD	H324T5

CUSTOMER

CustID	CustName	CustStreet	CustCity	CustState	CustZip	CustCLmt

When PRODUCT, PURCHASE_ORDER, and PO_LINE_ITEM are represented as tables in a relational database, we repeat the identifiers of

PRODUCT and PURCHASE_ORDER in PO_LINE_ITEM to indicate their relationships, as shown below with an instance of each entity:

PURCHASE_ORDER

PONumber	PODate	POAmt	POTerms	CustID
ABC9087-95	02/01/95	2046.98	debit acct	A187B3
PO17654	02/11/95	437.08	COD	H324T5

PO_LINE_ITEM

PONumber	PODate	ProdID	POLineQnty	POExtPrice
ABC9087-95	02/01/95	B91W	5	150.00
PO17654	02/11/95	S23Y	2	30.00

PRODUCT

ProdID	ProdDesc	ProdUnit	ProdPrice
B91W	Whatsit	case	30.00
S23Y	Widget	each	15.00

Notice that PO_LINE_ITEM now has three key identifiers—PONumber, PODate, and ProdID—all of which are needed to uniquely identify a line on a purchase order.[1] A key identifier of one entity used as an attribute of another entity is called a **foreign key**. Using foreign keys establishes a link between the tables, allowing us to produce reports that contain data from both. You might wonder how you can know that the key identifier of CUSTOMER should be used as a foreign key in PURCHASE_ORDER. Why isn't the key identifier of PURCHASE_ORDER used as a foreign key in CUSTOMER instead?

The answer to this question is derived from the fact that each cell (the intersection of a row and a column) in a table can contain only one data value. Recall that each customer can submit many purchase orders, but each row in the PURCHASE_ORDER table (that is, each instance of a purchase order) can have only one value in the CustID column. Thus, we can't use PONumber as a foreign key in CUSTOMER because we would have to store more than one value for PONumber in the PONumber cell for each customer. In contrast, each purchase order is submitted by *exactly one customer*. Therefore, we can store the CustID with each instance of a PURCHASE_ORDER without violating the one-data-value-per-cell rule.

---

[1] The fact that ProdID is a key identifier here indicates that each product can be listed only once on each purchase order.

Appendix DB2:
Linking Files and Creating Views

As explained in Appendix DB1, the tables of a relational database are related to each other by using the key identifier of one entity as a foreign key in its related entity. Whenever two tables share an attribute, we can join the tables to generate a report that contains data from both. When we implement these tables using a relational DBMS, each table is stored as a file. If we need to access data from two or more files to generate a report, we must first "tell" the DBMS how these files are related before we issue the command to generate the report.

The process for linking files in dBase III+ is described here. All of the dot prompt command procedures (e.g., as shown in #3 in the Process Summary) work in both dBASE III+ and dBASE IV; Assistant mode procedures work only in DBASE III+.

Process Summary

1. At the main dBase menu, select *Database* from the *Setup* menu; highlight the letter that represents the drive (probably A: or B:) containing the files you want to link.

2. Press [ESC] to move from the menu-based Assistant mode to dot prompt mode. The menus at the top of your screen will disappear, and a command line, indicated by a line beginning with a period or dot (.) will appear at the lower part of your screen.

3. To link two files, enter the following commands:

    SELECT 1
    USE <source file>
    SELECT 2
    USE <target file>
    INDEX ON <common field> **TO** <index file>
    SELECT 1
    SET RELATION TO <common field> **INTO** <target file>

where words enclosed in brackets < > indicate that you need to substitute the name of the appropriate file or field.

4. Enter the command to print your report.

Command Description

The **SELECT** command opens a new work area or activates a work area—that is, it indicates that the file stored in the selected work area is the one to be processed by the subsequent command. dBASE allows you to open several work areas at a time, but only one work area is active at any given time. An easy way to tell which file is active is to examine the status line at the bottom of your screen; the active file is the file whose name is displayed in the third column of the status line.

■ **Figure A-8**

Work Area

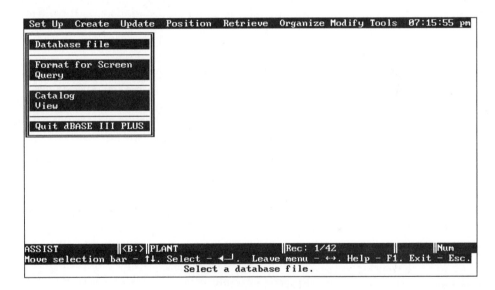

The **USE** command assigns the named file to the current work area. To link two files, each must be assigned to a work area. Here we assign the source file to work area 1 and the target file to work area 2. A **source file** is a file that will be processed to generate a report. Generally speaking, the source file is the one from which you will select records based on selection criteria or conditions. A **target file** is a file that is used to look up data that will be included in the report. The target file is accessed solely for the purpose of looking up data not available in the source file.

The **INDEX** command is required if the target file has not already been indexed using the common field as the index field. The **common field** is the field that is stored in both files. The **INDEX** command creates another file, an **index file,** that determines the order in which records in that file will be processed. The target file must be indexed on the common field before it can be linked to the source file. After you enter this command, dBASE will display the message "100% indexed # records indexed" where # will be replaced by the number of records in your target file.

The **SET RELATION** command specifies how the open files are related. The source file must be active—that is, currently selected—when this command is issued; the third **SELECT** command in the procedure above deactivates the target file and activates the source file. After issuing the **SET RELATION** command, you can verify that the files have been linked successfully by entering the **DISPLAY STATUS** command. This command will display the name and information about the file in each open work area.

■ **Figure A-9**

Display Status

```
. display status

Currently Selected Database:
Select area:   1, Database in Use: B:INTRSORT.DBF    Alias: INTRSORT

Select area:   2, Database in Use: B:BOOKS.DBF    Alias: BOOKS
      Master index file:   B:BOOKINT.NDX   Key: interest

File search path:
Default disk drive: B:
Print destination:   PRN:
Margin =        0
Current work area =     1

Press any key to continue...
Command Line        <B:> INTRSORT                    Rec: 1/8              Num

                Enter a dBASE III PLUS command.
```

Process Example

Let's walk through an example to illustrate the linking procedure. Assume that the database consists of two files: CUSTOMER and P_ORDER. Furthermore, assume that we want to generate a report listing the purchase order number, purchase order date, customer name, and purchase order amount for all customers who live in San Jose. The files and a sample record of each are shown on page 149.

In this example, the CUSTOMER file is the source file because it is the one being processed: we want the DBMS to include in our report only those records where the value for CustCity is "San Jose." P_ORDER is the target file because this table is being accessed solely for the purpose of looking up data

PURCHASE_ORDER

PONumber	PODate	POAmt	POTerms	CustID
ABC9087-95	02/01/95	2046.98	debit acct	A187B3
PO17654	02/11/95	437.08	COD	H324T5

CUSTOMER

CustID	CustName	CustStreet	CustCity	CustSt	CustZip	CustCLmt
A187B3	ABC Corp.	21 Industry	Milpitas	CA	95195	10,000.00
H324T5	Dan Harding	123 Elm St.	San Jose	CA	95193	5,000.00

values not available in the CUSTOMER file. The common field shared by these files is CustID. Thus, to link these files, we would use the following commands:

> **SELECT** 1
> **USE** customer
> **SELECT** 2
> **USE** p_order
> **INDEX ON** custid **TO** po_index
> **SELECT** 1
> **SET RELATION TO** custid **INTO** p_order

Once we have linked the files, we can enter the command to print the report. To do this from dot command mode, we would enter the command

> **LIST** p_order->ponumb, p_order->podate, custname, p_order->poamt
> **FOR** custcity ="San Jose" **TO PRINT**

Notice that fields from the target file include a prefix consisting of their file name and a connector composed of a hyphen followed by the greater-than symbol (->). This **target file prefix** is necessary in order to tell dBASE to retrieve these data values from an inactive file. To close all the open files, type **CLOSE ALL** at the dot prompt.

Process Extension: Linking Three Files

Some reports require that you link more than two files. For example, you may have one source file but two or more target files. As long as each pair of these files have a field in common, you can link them and generate a report listing data from all three. For example, assume that the database described above includes a third file, INVOICE.

P_ORDER

PONumber	PODate	POAmt	POTerms	CustID
ABC9087-95	02/01/95	2046.98	debit acct	A187B3
PO17654	02/11/95	437.08	COD	H324T5

CUSTOMER

CustID	CustName	CustStreet	CustCity	CustSt	CustZip	CustCLmt
A187B3	ABC Corp.	21 Industry	Milpitas	CA	95195	10,000.00
H324T5	Dan Harding	123 Elm St.	San Jose	CA	95193	5,000.00

INVOICE

InvNumb	PONumb	CustID	InvAmt
PN372	ABC9087-95	A187B3	2046.98
TC008	PO17654	H324T5	437.08

Notice that both the P_ORDER file and the INVOICE file are related to CUSTOMER by the common field CustID; P_ORDER is also related to INVOICE by the common field PONumb.

Given these relationships among the three files, you can link them to generate a report that, for example, lists the customer name, purchase order date, and invoice number for all invoices with a total amount greater than $500. In this example, INVOICE is the source file because records will be selected from this file based on their InvAmt values. CUSTOMER and P_ORDER are target files that are accessed only to look up data values to be printed. INVOICE is related into P_ORDER on PONumb, and then P_ORDER is related into CUSTOMER on Custid as shown below:

```
SELECT 1
USE invoice
SELECT 2
USE p_order
INDEX ON ponumb TO poind
SELECT 1
SET RELATION TO ponumb INTO p_order
SELECT 3
USE customer
INDEX ON custid TO custind
SELECT 2
SET RELATION TO custid INTO customer
```

To display the report, you would first make the source file INVOICE active and then issue the **LIST** command:

SELECT 1
LIST customer->custname, p_order->podate, invnumb **FOR** invamt > 20

Process Short-Cut: Creating and Using a View File

If the linked files are commonly used to generate reports, you can avoid having to repeat the linking process each time you want to generate a report by creating a view file. A **view** **file** is a file that contains the specifications of a particular database environment: the names of the open database and index files, the work areas in which these files are located, the relationships established among these files, and so on.

To create a view file of your current work environment, go into dot prompt mode and enter the command

CREATE VIEW <view filename> **FROM ENVIRONMENT**

where <view filename> is substituted by the name of your view file, e.g., custord to indicate that this view links the CUSTOMER and PURCHASE-ORDER files. dBASE automatically adds the extension **.VUE** to your view file name. You can also create a view file in the menu-based Assistant mode, but we recommend that you use dot commands to link files and then issue the **CREATE VIEW** command to create a view file.

To use a view file, you must first open it. You can open a view file in one of two ways. In dot command mode, enter the following command:

SET VIEW TO <view filename>

Or, if you're working in the menu-based Assistant mode, select *View* from the *Create* menu, highlight the desired view file, and press [Enter].

Appendix DB3:
Creating a Report Format File

To specify your own report layout, you need to create a **report format file** that defines your report's titles, headings, columns, and fields. The procedure described here assumes that you are using dBASE III+; if you are using dBASE IV or another DBMS, *consult your user manual.*

As you enter your report format specifications, you can verify them by consulting the Report Format box in the middle of the screen. This box displays the current layout of your report.

Important note: Be sure that the file to be used in your report is active before creating your report format. If your report will contain data from two files, you will need to set the view before creating your report format. See Appendix DB2 for information about creating and using views.

■ **Figure A-10**

Report Format Screen

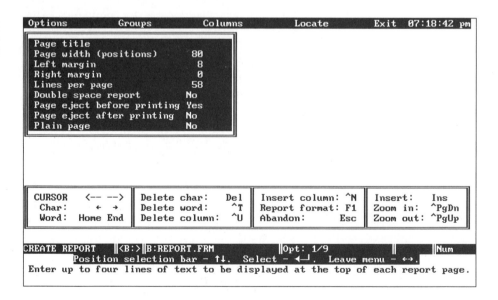

Accessing the Report Format Option

1a. Select *Report* from the *Create* menu. Enter the name you want to assign to your report format file.

1b. If you prefer to work in dot command mode, press [Esc] to leave Assistant mode and then enter the following command:

CREATE REPORT <reportname>

replacing <reportname> with the name of your report format file.

2. The Report Format screen will appear. To select options from the Report Format menu, use your cursor movement keys to highlight the desired option, and then press [Enter].

Specifying a Title for Your Report

1a. Normally, when you enter the command for creating a report format, the Report Format screen will open with *Options* already highlighted and the cursor (a solid triangle) located at the *Page Title* option. Press [Enter] to select this option and enter a title.

1b. If the Options menu is not already open, select *Options* from the Report Format menu. At the Options submenu, select *Page Title.* A window will appear to the right of the Options submenu.

2. Enter up to four lines for your title. As you finish typing each line, press [Enter] to advance to the next line.

3. When you're finished entering the title, press [Ctrl] [End] to return to the *Options* submenu.

Creating a Report with Subtotals

1. Select *Groups* from the Report Format menu.

2. Select *Group on expression* from the *Groups* submenu. A cursor will appear; enter the name of the **grouping field,** the field on which to group records, or press [F10] to select a field name from a displayed list.

3. To indicate a group heading, select *Group heading,* and enter your desired heading.

4. The other *Groups* formatting options include *Summary report only* (where *no* indicates that you want both group totals and a grand total; *yes* indicates that you want only group totals) and *Page eject after group* (where *yes* indicates that you want each group printed on a separate page). You can change the setting for one of these options by highlighting it and pressing [Enter].

Defining Columns in Your Report

1. Select *Columns* from the Report Format menu. A window will appear, in which you will enter the *contents* (i.e., field name), *heading,* and *width* for each of your columns. To keep track of what column you are entering, consult the "Column:" memo in the status bar at the bottom of the screen.

■ **Figure A-11**

Column Options Window

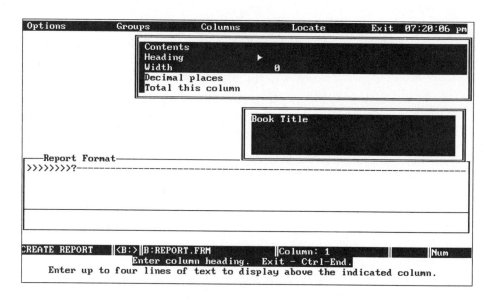

2. To begin defining a column, select the *Contents* option. At the cursor, enter the name of the field you want displayed in your first column— or press [F10] to see a list of field names, and select the desired field from the list. If you are including fields from two files, you will need to use a prefix when specifying fields from the target file:

\<name of target file> -> \<name of field>

3. Next, select the *Heading* option; a Heading window will open in which you can enter up to four lines for your heading, pressing [Enter] at the end of each line. When you have finished entering the heading for your first column, press [Ctrl] [End] to close the Heading window and return to the *Columns* option window.

4. When you entered a field name in the *Contents* option, dBASE automatically assigned that field's width and decimal places as the default values for the *Width* and *Decimal* places options. If you want to change these, select the option, and enter your own value.

5. Finally, if you want to *total this column*, be sure that *yes* appears as the value for this option. You can toggle from *yes* to *no* to *yes* by high-lighting the option and pressing [Enter].

6. When you have finished defining one report column, press [PageDown] to advance to a blank column entry window. Repeat the column definition process for each column in your report. To go back to an earlier column entry to modify it, press [PageUp].

Modifying a Report Format

1a. If you are working in Assistant mode, at the main dBASE menu, select *Modify*. At the Modify submenu, select *Report*.

1b. If you are working in dot command mode, enter the MODIFY REPORT command:

MODIFY REPORT <reportname>

2. Follow the procedures outlined above to modify your title, columns, etc.

Saving Your Report Format File

1. Select *Exit* from the Report Format menu.

2. When the Exit submenu opens, select *Save* if you want to save your report; select *Abandon* if you want to exit without saving. The Report Format menu disappears, and you are returned to the dot prompt.

Using Your Report Format

1. If you are in the menu-based Assistant mode, select *Report* from the *Retrieve* menu. Select the appropriate drive and file from the displayed lists.

2. If you are in dot command mode, at the dot prompt, enter the REPORT FORM command in the following syntax:

REPORT FORM <reportname> TO PRINT

where the name of your report format file is substituted for <reportname>.

If you want to specify that only certain records should be printed, add the FOR clause:

REPORT FORM <reportname> FOR <condition> TO PRINT

where your selection condition (e.g., inv_status = 'is') is substituted for <condition>.

Troubleshooting

Here are a few troubleshooting suggestions in case you run into problems creating a report.

1. If you are creating a report that accesses just one file, was that file active before you began creating your report? Check the status line to be sure that the file name is displayed before you begin creating your report.

2. If you are creating a report that accesses two files, was the view linking those two files active before you began creating your report? Did you remember to use a prefix on the fields to be accessed from your target file? Also, you may need to verify that you specified the source and target files correctly in your view file.

3. If you tried to group report lines on a particular field but the lines were not grouped correctly in the report, you may need to sort the file containing the grouping field before creating your view and/or report format files. Sort the file on the grouping field, and then use the sorted file, not the regular file, as you create your view and/or report format files. The **SORT** command in dBASE is

SORT ON <primary sort key field> **TO** <filename>

where <primary sort key field> is the field used to sort the records.

4. If some of the records you expected in your report weren't displayed, verify that you specified the condition value correctly and that the values contained in the relevant fields were entered correctly. For example, assume that you want to see a book report (bkrpt.frm) of all

books written by Hemingway; but to generate your report, you issued the command

REPORT FORM bkrpt **FOR** author = "hemigway"

Your typing error is obviously the problem here! Similarly, if some of the books by Hemingway were listed, but others weren't, you should edit your book file to make sure that you spelled Hemingway correctly as you specified values for the author field.

Appendix DB4:
Miscellaneous Database Procedures

Writing Queries with Compound Conditions

In dBASE, you can specify multiple query conditions in the **FOR** statement by using the logical operators **.AND.** and **.OR.** to join the conditions. For example,

> **LIST** .... **FOR** <condition1> **.and.** <condition2>
> **LIST** .... **FOR** <condition1> **.or.** <condition2>

The first command lists all records that satisfy both conditions; the second command lists all records that satisfy at least one of the conditions.

Creating a Label Format File

It's quite easy to create a label format file using dBASE's Assistant mode. Before you begin the following procedure, make sure that your customer file is active.

1. Select *Label* from the *Create* menu.

2. Indicate a drive on which to store your file, and then enter a file name. dBASE automatically adds the extension **.LBL** to your file name.

3. The label format screen will appear with the Options window open. In this window, you specify the characteristics of the mailing label form you are using. We'll accept the default label specifications, which allow you to enter up to 5 lines for each mailing label. Just use your cursor movement keys to highlight the second selection on the Labels menu, *Contents*. Press [Enter] to open the *Contents* window.

4. Select line 1 (highlight and press [Enter]); a triangular cursor will appear.

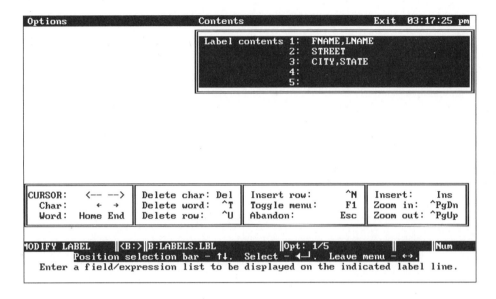

■ **Figure A-12**

Contents Window

5. Press [F10] to see a list of the fields in your customer file. Use your cursor movement keys to highlight the first field you want displayed on line 1. Press [Enter]. The selected field name will appear after the cursor. If you want more than one field printed on a line, type a comma (,) and then select the second field name.

6. When you have finished entering field names for line 1, press [Enter]. The triangular cursor will disappear, signaling that you have completed specifying line 1.

7. Use your cursor movement keys to move to line 2. Press [Enter]. Repeat Steps 5 and 6 for each line of your label.

8. When you have finished defining the label format, select *Exit* and then *Save* to save your label format file.

9. To generate your labels, select *Label* from the *Retrieve* menu. Indicate the drive, file name, and print destination, when prompted by dBASE.

Vocabulary Index